T0322981

SHARI'AH COMPLIANT PRIVATE EQUITY AND ISLAMIC VENTURE CAPITAL

Edinburgh Guides to Islamic Finance
Series Editor: Rodney Wilson

A series of short guides to key areas in Islamic finance, offering an independent academic perspective and a critical treatment.

Product Development in Islamic Banks
Habib Ahmed

Shari'ah *Compliant Private Equity and Islamic Venture Capital*
Fara Madehah Ahmad Farid

Shari'ah *Governance in Islamic Banks*
Zulkifli Hasan

Islamic Financial Services in the United Kingdom
Elaine Housby

Islamic Asset Management
Natalie Schoon

Legal, Regulatory and Governance Issues in Islamic Finance
Rodney Wilson

Forthcoming
Islamic and Ethical Finance in the United Kingdom
Elaine Housby

www.euppublishing.com/series/egif

SHARI'AH COMPLIANT PRIVATE EQUITY AND ISLAMIC VENTURE CAPITAL

Fara Madehah Ahmad Farid

EDINBURGH
University Press

I am grateful to Allah (swt) for the completion of this book. Special thanks are forwarded to Professor Rodney Wilson for his expertise, knowledge and guidance. Thank you to my beloved husband and mother for their tremendous support.

© Fara Madehah Ahmad Farid, 2012

Edinburgh University Press Ltd
22 George Square, Edinburgh EH8 9LF
www.euppublishing.com

Typeset in Minion Pro by
Servis Filmsetting Ltd, Stockport, Cheshire, and
printed and bound in Great Britain by
CPI Group (UK) Ltd, Croydon CR0 4YY

A CIP record for this book is available from the British Library

ISBN 978 0 7486 4047 8 (hardback)
ISBN 978 0 7486 4048 5 (paperback)
ISBN 978 0 7486 5561 8 (webready PDF)
ISBN 978 0 7486 5563 2 (epub)
ISBN 978 0 7486 5562 5 (Amazon ebook)

The right of Fara Madehah Ahmad Farid to be identified as author of this work has been asserted in accordance with the Copyright, Designs and Patents Act 1988.

CONTENTS

TABLES

FIGURES

CHAPTER 1
GROWTH AND PROSPECTS OF ISLAMIC BANKING AND FINANCE IN THE MENA AND ASEAN REGIONS

During the time of Prophet Muhammad (saw), *mudhārabah* was a form of sale contract used by the trade merchants to finance trade over long distances. Islamic finance then evolved into a wider context during the reign of Umar Al-Khattab's caliphate when pension and welfare benefits were introduced. Trade was always encouraged among Muslims during the prime of the Islamic civilisation as it creates wealth, opportunities and increased charity for mankind in the name of the Almighty Allah (swt). In addition the specific portion of income generated is given to the poor and this is called *zakat*. This shows that the existence of a small-business entity is not only for profit but also to assist the poor in terms of charity and opportunity.

The point highlighted here is that these trade and business transactions carried out by the Prophet and his companions were abiding by Islamic law and the business contract was formed on a partnership basis, the *mudhārabah*. As more modern and sophisticated elements of economic principles evolve, trade and commerce that adhere to Islamic law, that is, Islamic banking and finance, slowly develop and compete with the market in the business sector. Segments of Islamic banking and finance to date are categorised according to business areas such as:

- commercial banking
- trade finance
- capital market
- investment banking, and
- private equity (PE) and venture capital

Figure 1.1 shows a more detailed evolution of Islamic financial products, starting from their inception in the 1970s.

Referring to Figure 1.1, Islamic financial instruments have expanded to cover business areas other than commercial banking. Although capital market products are still in their infancy and hedging tools are small in number, the market for them is desirable because Islamic financial instruments need to remain competitive with the existing conventional financial instruments. The ISDA (International Swaps and Derivatives Association) and the IIFM (International Islamic Financial Market) collaborated to structure a standardised document for hedging purposes and to comply with *Shari'ah* rules. 'The ISDA/IIFM Tahawwut Master Agreement provides the structure under which institutions can transact Islamic hedging transactions such as profit-rate and currency swaps, which are estimated to represent most of today's Islamic hedging transactions.'[1] This technique of Islamic hedging makes the Islamic banking industry competitive and increases confidence in the market for Islamic products and businesses. It also helps in managing risks efficiently.

In addition, new Islamic financial instruments engineered for liquidity, risk management and private equity

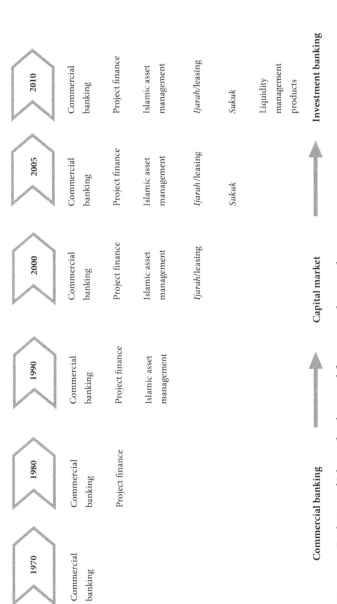

1970	1980	1990	2000	2005	2010
Commercial banking	Commercial banking	Commercial banking	Commercial banking	Commercial banking	Commercial banking
	Project finance	Project finance	Project finance	Project finance	Project finance
		Islamic asset management	Islamic asset management	Islamic asset management	Islamic asset management
			Ijarah/leasing	*Ijarah*/leasing	*Ijarah*/leasing
				Sukuk	*Sukuk*
					Liquidity management products

Commercial banking   **Capital market**   **Investment banking**

Figure 1.1 *Evolution of Islamic banking and finance products and services*

were the highlights from 2000 onwards. Commodity *murabaha* is an example of an Islamic financial instrument used for liquidity-management purposes. Although there are concerns pertaining to *Shari'ah* compliancy, commodity *murabaha* has an annual turnover of over US$1 trillion.[2] However, the challenge remains for other Islamic financial instruments for liquidity-management purposes in terms of *Shari'ah* compliancy. Private equity and venture capital is one of the latest innovations in Islamic banking and finance. For example, the Islamic leveraged buyout (LBO) structure of the buyout of Aston Martin paved the way for structuring Islamic financial instruments that were more innovative.

1.1 Theory and application of Islamic banking and finance

The structures of Islamic banking and finance products are taken from *Shari'ah* law, Islamic law which is taken from the Al-Quran and the *sunnah*, that is, from the example and lifestyle of Prophet Muhammad (saw). In *Shari'ah* law there are classifications of contracts in the categories of asset ownership exchange, the sale and use of usufruct, partnership based on profit and loss sharing, trusts, security and agency. These categories are the theory that is applied in structuring Islamic financial products. Tables 1.1 to 1.5 show the products under each category.

Shari'ah compliant private equity and Islamic venture capital fall under the partnership category. In Islamic law, partnership, in Arabic *shirkah*, is further developed into several other types of partnership. *Shirkah* is more frequently used in Islamic jurisprudence and all these modes of sharing or partnership are termed as *shirkah* in *fiqh*.[3] *Shirkah* according to Islamic law is further discussed in Chapter 3.

Table 1.1 *Asset ownership exchange contracts*

bai al-arbun	A down payment on a sales contract. The full price of the goods purchased is not fully paid and the buyer has not taken possession of the goods yet. If the buyer does not purchase the goods, the down payment will be forfeited. For example, if customer A wants to buy a car and makes a down payment of £1,000 for a car costing £15,000, she will later pay £14,000 if she decides to go through with the purchase. If she decides not to purchase the car, the £1,000 is forfeited. *Arbun* is mainly used as an option for hedging purposes.
bai al-inah	This refers to the selling of an asset by the bank to the customer through deferred payments. At a later date, the bank will repurchase the asset. In a *bai al-inah* contract the transfer of ownership of the asset is on paper only.
bai al-istisna	A contract whereby both parties agree on manufacturing goods and commodities. The payment is made in advance and the goods and commodities delivered at a future date. Similar to *salam* financing, the buyer needs to get all the information concerning the goods to be manufactured. Payments can be done in installments as agreed by the parties involved. *Istisna* can be used for financing the construction of houses, plants, roads, and so on.

Table 1.1 *continued*

bai al-salam	*Salam* is a contract whereby payment is done in advance and the goods are delivered later. According to *Shari'ah* law, the goods have to be in existence while transactions take place. However, in the case of *salam* financing there are some exceptions. The buyer needs to receive all the information about the goods and the delivery date should be fixed. In this contract, the seller sells the goods to the buyer at a future date but for a price agreed and paid at the time the contract takes place.
bai bithamin ajil	A cost-plus sale type of financing mode and mainly used on a short-term basis – for example the hire-purchase of a vehicle. *Murabaha* is used for long-term financing.
murabaha	A cost-plus sale type of financing mode. The Islamic bank will buy the asset on behalf of the borrower and sell it to the borrower at a mark-up price. The selling price depends on the profit rate of the Islamic bank. For example, if the price of the house is £100,000, the Islamic bank will buy the house at £100,000 and sell it to the borrower at £125,000 at a profit rate of 25%.

Table 1.2 *Sale and use of usufruct contracts*

ijarah	A leasing type of financing mode. Islamic banks lease equipment and buildings at an agreed rental to the client. This is similar to that of an operating lease.

Table 1.2 *continued*

ijarah wa iqtina	A leasing type of financing mode with the option to purchase the asset by the lessee at the end of the leasing period. For example, Islamic banks buy vans from vendor A and enter into a two-year contract with customer B (lessee) who will be using the vans for his catering business. Customer B will be paying a monthly rent for two years and when the lease ends the title of ownership of the vans will be transferred to customer B.

Table 1.3 *Partnership contracts*

mudhārabah	A partnership type of financing mode with a profit- and loss-sharing feature. Profit is determined based on a profit rate agreed by partners. Losses are borne by the investor and the entrepreneur only manages the business.
mushārakah	A partnership type of financing mode with a profit- and loss-sharing feature. Profit is determined based on the profit rate agreed by partners. Losses are determined based on the capital invested into the partnership. All partners share the management of the business. For example, Rachid and Iman are partners and entered into a *mushārakah* contract. Both agreed that the profit will be shared according to the ratio 1:3. The company made a profit of £100,000. Rachid receives £25,000 and Iman receives £75,000.

Table 1.4 *Trusts contracts*

rahn	*Rahn* means to pledge a property that has value as a security for debt. The creditor will recover the debt from the property in case the debtor cannot pay back in time.
wadiah	In the *wadiah*, customers deposit money in the bank and the bank is totally responsible and liable for its safekeeping. It is safekeeping with a guarantee. It is commonly used in Islamic banks in Malaysia.

Table 1.5 *Security contracts and contracts to carry out a specific activity or project*

hawalah	A contract which consists of transfer of debt from one party to another. This transfer is via an intermediary. For example, a debt is transferred by person A to person B whereby A will be free of the debt and B becomes responsible for it.
juala (commission)	A contract to assign a task to another party who agrees to carry out the task agreed with a commission or a fee.
wakalah (agency)	A contract of agency whereby one is appointed to carry out a certain task by the contractor (banks). For example, mutual funds and brokerage services who are the agent (*wakil*) for the Islamic banks.

1.2 Statistics and development

In this section, statistics from 2000 to 2008 are reviewed in order to analyse the evolution of the Islamic banking and finance industry. This will provide an insight into the opportunities and challenges for the Islamic banking and finance industry as well as for *Shari'ah* compliant private equity funds. (The absence of statistics from 2008 onwards does not necessarily negate the usefulness of the information.)

> The silver lining for the industry is the continued strong growth in the overall *Shari'ah* sensitive investable assets. Ashar Nazim, Director at Ernst & Young's Islamic Financial Services team in Bahrain says: 'The *Shari'ah* compliant investable wealth pool grew by 20 per cent to reach US$ 480 Bn in 2009. In 2008, this was US$ 400 Bn. The GCC [Gulf Cooperation Council] emains the single biggest contributor to this growing wealth pool. It clearly represents substantial untapped opportunities for local and international players who can understand and respond to their investors' evolving needs.'[4]

This quotation gives an indication of the immense wealth in the GCC and the Middle East, where it can be channelled for the development of the Islamic banking and finance industry and in pursuit of global business partnerships. This can be seen through the emergence of *Shari'ah* compliant private equity funds, the high volume of *sukuk* issuance, as well as Islamic funds and Islamic hedging. This boosts the total assets and capital for most of the existing Islamic financial institutions and at the same time diversifies the products and services available. At present the retail banking sector comprises most of the services of the Islamic financial institution worldwide. However, changes are crucial to be competitive and mark a global positioning to capture markets worldwide.

Based on the World Islamic Banking Competitiveness Report 2011–12 provided by Ernst & Young, Islamic banking assets with commercial banks globally will reach US$1.1 trillion in 2012. This was US$826 billion in 2010.[5] This is a tremendous increase.

The Middle East and Malaysia are the key leaders in this industry along with several other countries with potential growth such as the United Kingdom, France, the United States of America, Turkey and Indonesia. The development of the Islamic banking and finance industry does not necessarily mean that it should be developed in Muslim countries only. The United Kingdom demonstrates that Islamic banking and finance can play a major role in the financial sector in a non-Muslim country. Aside from providing the market to its Muslim population, Islamic banking and finance also contributes to the country's economy in terms of raising capital and increasing liquidity through a high volume of transactions using Islamic banking and finance products worldwide.

Between 2000 and 2007 the global assets of Islamic finance increased substantially. In 2006, the global asset of Islamic finance was US$397 billion, increasing to US$537 billion in 2007.[6] This is for commercial banks only. Commercial banks are the key players in the Islamic banking and finance industry, placing themselves in the global competitive market. Some of the largest Islamic banks are Al-Rajhi Bank, Dubai Islamic Bank and Kuwait Finance House. The largest Islamic bank in the world is Al-Rajhi Bank, established in 1987 in Riyadh, Saudi Arabia; it had US$43.5 billion in assets in 2008. The primary banking products are retail and provide financing for small and medium-sized enterprises (SMEs).

In the United Arab Emirates, Dubai Islamic Bank is one of the largest in the region, with AED85 billion in assets in December 2008. Most of the incomes are generated from Islamic financing and investing activities, investments in *sukuk* and international *murabaha* on a short-term basis.[7]

Investment banking meanwhile builds US$85 billion of the overall global assets of Islamic finance. This demonstrates the fast rate of growth of *Shari'ah* compliant private equity funding in the Middle East and in Asia, mainly in Malaysia, which is active in promoting Islamic private equity and venture capital. Table 1.6 shows a list of private equity companies in the Middle East. In addition, the CIMB Group, Malaysia's largest investment bank, which includes CIMB Islamic, has a private equity subsidiary. It focuses on medium- and long-term investments, often for five years or more.

Table 1.6 *Leading Gulf-based private equity funds*[8]

Location	Company	Conventional or *Shari'ah* board
Bahrain	Arcapita	Conventional
Bahrain	Investcorp	Conventional
Doha	Corecap	*Shari'ah* board
Dubai	Abrajj Capital	Conventional
Dubai	Millennium Private Equity	*Shari'ah* board
Dubai	Shuaa Capital	*Shari'ah* board
Kuwait	Gulf Finance House	Conventional
Kuwait	Investment Dar	*Shari'ah* board
Kuwait	NBK Capital	Conventional
Riyadh	Swicorp	Appointing *Shari'ah* board

Source: Rodney Wilson, 2009.

Sukuk is also a major part of the global assets in Islamic banking and finance. In 2006, the *sukuk* issue was US\$66 billion and it increased to US\$85 billion in 2007.[9] The demand for *sukuk* is gaining momentum, with other countries like France and Russia showing interest in Islamic banking and finance. Al-Shams Capital, an investment and financial company incorporated in Russia, is paving the way with Islamic banking products and services in Russia. Al-Shams Capital foresees that there is demand for Islamic banking services and products such as retail, investment, *takaful* and *sukuk*.[10] *Sukuk* issuance also plays a major role in positioning the Islamic banking industry side by side with the conventional banking and bond markets.

If we analyse the figures by country, the Middle East, Malaysia and GCC countries remain the key players in the Islamic banking and finance industry. The United Kingdom, on the other hand, is a key player in Europe. According to Taxprecision, 'At the end of 2011 there are \$19 billion of Shari'ah compliant assets in the United Kingdom and \$1 trillion globally with a potential of growth to \$4 trillion.'[11]

1.3 Growth and future prospects

There are around one billion Muslims, including 40.7 per cent of the population of Africa and 20.2 per cent of the population of Asia. About ten million Muslims live in North America and Europe.[12] These population figures provide Muslims with the opportunity to conduct trade, commerce and savings in an Islamic manner through Islamic banking and finance. Malaysia, for example, has established a dual banking system, regulated by the Central Bank of Malaysia.

Based on the World Islamic Banking Competitiveness Report 2011–12 provided by Ernst & Young, the Middle East and North Africa (MENA) Islamic banking industry is projected to be worth $990 billion by 2015. In 2010 the assets were $416 billion.[13] Demand for the product contributes to this growth whereby the wealth in the GCC region is increasing and further expanding the Islamic banking and finance industry, making it attractive to investors abroad. This is proven due to the existence of the industry in non-Muslim countries such as the United Kingdom, France and Germany to name but three.

In Indonesia there is huge potential for expanding the Islamic banking and finance industry due to a large market, beneficial for both Muslims and non-Muslims.

According to the CPI financial news on 8th of May 2012, Halim Alamsyah who is the Deputy Governor of the Bank of Indonesia, mentioned that 'Indonesia's Islamic finance assets were worth IDR 214 trillion ($23.2 billion), of which around 69.5 per cent are banking assets. Indonesia has 11 Shari'ah-compliant commercial banks, 24 Shari'ah bank business units and 155 Shari'ah-compliant rural banks (Bank Perkreditan Rakyat) with total assets of IDR 152.3 trillion (about US$16.5 billion).'[14]

Furthermore, the ranges of products offered by the Islamic banks have diverted into other areas of the banking sector. Investment banking is on the rise, together with real estate, project financing and hedge funds.

Aside from products, most Islamic banks provide services, including e-banking, telephone banking and other high-tech products, for the convenience of the consumer. Islamic banks are placing themselves within the global market and staying competitive within the overall banking industry. The rate of growth for the Islamic banking and finance industry shows that the market is expanding. This means that the key players need to remain competitive and create new products and services. The existing products and services need to be improved in terms of customer satisfaction. There are many financial reasons for developing further and improving the Islamic banking and financial industry whereby it assists in creating wealth through small businesses, which then creates employment for the entire economy.

Notes

1. 'IIFM and ISDA launch tahawwut (hedging) master agreement', http://www.isda.org/media/press/2010/press030 110.html (retrieved 9 November 2010).

2. 'Liquidity management in Islamic capital markets', *Islamic Business and Finance*, 2010, http://www.zawya.com/story. cfm?id=ZAWYA20100620120228 (retrieved 10 August 2011).

3. Muhammad Taqi Usmani, *An Introduction to Islamic Finance* (Alphen aan den Rijn: Kluwer Law International, 2002), p. 5.

4. 'Oman to add US$6bn in Islamic assets, says Ernst & Young', http://www.zawya.com/sukuk/story.cfm/sidZAWYA20110 609050421/Oman_to_add_6bn_in_Islamic_assets_says_ Ernst __Young (retrieved 9 November 2010).

5. World Islamic Banking Conference, 21–3 November 2011, Bahrain, http://www.sesric.org/event-detail.php?id=641 (retrieved 13 April 2012).

6. IFSL Research, 'Islamic Finance 2009', http://www.thecityuk. com/assets/Uploads/Islamic-finance-2009.pdf (retrieved 9 November 2010).

7. Dubai Islamic Bank PJSC (2009), p. 3, http://ae.zawya. com/cm/financials/5515_20090630_6_U_.pdf (retrieved 9 November 2010).

8. Rodney Wilson, 'Shariah compliant private equity finance', in Sohail Jaffer (ed.), *Islamic Wealth Management* (London: Euromoney Books, 2009), pp. 399–412.

9. Dubai Islamic Bank PJSC (2009), p. 15.

10. 'Al-Shams CEO eyes promoting Islamic finance in Russia', 8 March 2010, http://www.cibafi.org/NewsCenter/English/Details.aspx?Id=7194&Cat=0 (retrieved 12 February 2011).

11. Tax Precision: The International Tax Forum, 'UK to remain top financial hub in Europe', http://www.taxprecision.com/2011/12/articles/taxprecision-news/uk-to-remain-top-islamic-financial-hub-in-europe (retrieved 4 February 2012).

12. Salahuddin Ahmed, *Islamic Banking and Insurance: A Global Overview* (Kuala Lumpur: AS Noordeen, 2009), p. 14.

13. Ernst & Young, World Islamic Banking Competitiveness Report 2011–12, *A Brave New World of Sustainable Growth*, p. 5.

14. Robin Amlôt, 'Islamic finance grows more than 40 per cent a year, Bank Indonesia seminar told', 8 May 2012, http://www.cpifinancial.net/news/post/13890/islamic-finance-grows-more-than-40-per-cent-a-year-bank-indonesia-seminar-told (retrieved 8 May 2012).

CHAPTER 2

PRIVATE EQUITY AND VENTURE CAPITAL INDUSTRY IN THE MENA AND ASEAN REGIONS

This chapter looks at the performance and investments of private equity and venture capital in the ASEAN (Association of Southeast Asian Nations) and MENA (Middle East and North Africa) regions and provides an overview of small and medium-sized enterprises (SMEs) in these two regions as well as sources of private equity and venture capital, sectors of investment and private equity, and venture capital contributions to the regions.

In the ASEAN region, analysis of the Malaysian venture capital industry is highlighted due to its rapid development in Islamic venture capital and *Shari'ah* compliant private equity funds. As for the MENA region, emphasis is placed on the Middle East. The statistics included in this chapter may not necessarily include the most recent (those for 2011 to 2012). However, these statistics, mainly from the years 2000 to 2008, are chosen to develop an analysis of the private equity and venture capital industry in the ASEAN and MENA region with a focus on specific countries and regions where the industry is already developed. This will give an overview of where the industry is heading and how to develop it further.

Islamic venture capital has been introduced in Malaysia and is catching up with other venture capital funds, as is the case with *Shari'ah* compliant private equity in the MENA region, with huge opportunities available due to economic growth and the high price of oil.

2.1 Private equity and venture capital investment and performance

This section looks at private equity and venture capital development in Southeast Asia, the Middle East region and several countries in the emerging economy. A 2008 Deloitte report 'Hidden Treasures: Private Equity Business in ASEAN' highlights Vietnam as an attractive destination for private equity investment due to the privatisation of state-owned enterprises (SOEs).[1] It also states, 'Singapore and Malaysia have always attracted private equity investments in the manufacturing sector due to the availability of high quality business infrastructure, developed and open financial markets, and a stable political climate.'[2] These factors are also vital to further developing Islamic venture capital and *Shari'ah* compliant private equity. CMIA Capital Partners of Singapore launched a US$200 million (S$245.4 million) private equity fund that will invest in China and Southeast Asia.[3]

The venture capital and private equity industry in Malaysia has expanded since 2003 and is becoming one of the main sources of finance. Table 2.1 provides an overview of the development of the venture capital industry in Malaysia.

According to the Bank Negara Malaysia's Annual Report 2002, the number of venture capital companies in Malaysia rose from 41 to 46 at the end of 2002. The Malaysian government had stakes in nineteen, reflecting the important role

Table 2.1 *Venture capital industry in Malaysia (2003–4)*

	As at end 2003	As at end 2004
Venture capital funds (RM million)	2,118.1	2,266.0
Total investment (RM million)	878.7	1,058.0
No. of venture capital companies/funds	43	38
No. of venture capital fund management companies	31	34
No. of investee companies	298	332

Source: Bank Negara Malaysia Annual Report 2004.

Table 2.2 *Venture capital industry in Malaysia (2007–8)*

	As at end 2007	As at end 2008
Venture capital funds (RM million)	3,308.0	4,570.0
Total investment (RM million)	1,784.0	1,929.0
No. of venture capital companies/funds	52	56
No. of venture capital fund management companies	46	52
No. of investee companies	433	450

Source: Malaysian Venture Capital and Private Equity Directory 2009.

of the Malaysian government in promoting the growth of the venture capital industry.[4] Among the balance of eleven venture capital companies without government shareholding, nine were subsidiaries of financial institutions. In terms of participation from non-residents, nine, or 30 per cent, of the 30 venture capital companies had some form of foreign shareholding. From the nine, only one venture capital company had a majority foreign stake.[5]

There were slight fluctuations in the number of venture capital and venture capital management companies in 2003 and 2004. However, total investment increased compared to previous years, which shows the importance of venture capital financing in Malaysia. Total available funds for venture capital investments grew by 7 per cent to RM2.3 billion.[6] Total investments increased slightly by RM62.1 million at the end of 2004, amounting to RM289.3 million, which is not an aggressive jolt. This shows that the venture capital industry in Malaysia was moving at a slow pace and making a small percentage contribution to the gross domestic product (GDP).

By 2007 there was no doubt that the government was focusing on the venture capital and private equity industries. This was also due to the emergence of Islamic private equity and high liquidity in the MENA region, where investors were looking for an avenue in which to invest. At the end of 2007 the amount of investment was RM1.784 billion, increasing to RM1.929 billion in 2008. The number of investee companies also increased, from 433 in 2007 to 450 in 2008. The number of venture capital fund management companies showed a large increase, from 46 in 2007 to 52 in 2008. In terms of the stages of financing, Table 2.3 shows that 36.6 per cent of the investments made during 2004 were in the expansion/growth stage.

Investments in the seed capital stage and start-up capital stage in 2004 accounted for only 5.6 and 6.7 per cent respectively. These figures represent a slow increase compared to the previous years. Although this stage of financing is considered very risky, this increase in percentage shows the venture capitalists were slowly becoming less risk averse. In 2005 the percentage share reduced, with an increase in the later stages: expansion/growth, bridge, mezzanine, and pre-IPO (initial public offering). However, the focus is still

Table 2.3 *Investment by stage (2004 and 2005)*

Investment by stage (2004)			Investment by stage (2005)	
Business stage	RM million	% share	RM million	% share
Seed capital	16.1	5.6	11,643.1	2.7
Start-up capital	19.3	6.7	25,116.0	5.8
Early stage	48.9	16.9	107,276.3	24.9
Expansion/growth	105.8	36.6	61,569.0	14.3
Bridge, mezzanine, pre-IPO	67.2	23.2	162,204.8	37.6
Management buyout	19.2	6.6	29,664.0	6.9
Management buy-in	*data not available*	*data not available*	14,700.0	3.4
Cashing out (secondary purchase)	0.6	0.2	1,642.0	0.4
Other types of investment	12.1	4.2	17,748.0	4.1
Total	**289.4**	**100.0**	**431,563.2**	**100.0**

Source: Bank Negara Malaysia Annual Report 2004 and 2005.

upon the early stage investment. Several government grants were established for small and medium-scale enterprises that require financing, particularly at the early stage.

Bridge, mezzanine and pre-IPO come in second place with 23.2 per cent in 2004 and 37.6 per cent in 2005, which shows that investors are comfortable financing this stage because risks are not too high and at this stage the companies are geared to exit. In terms of outstanding investments by stage, the expansion/growth, bridge, mezzanine, pre-IPO and start-up capital stages received the bulk of venture capital investments after 2002.[7] This shows an emphasis on both venture capital financing and private equity financing.

Table 2.4 *Investment by stage (2008).*

Business stage	RM million	% share	Number of investee companies
Seed capital	12,757	3	31
Start-up capital	3,000	1	3
Early stage	82,785	17	21
Expansion/growth	298,632	62	65
Bridge, mezzanine, pre-IPO	60,366	13	11
Management buy-in	11,500	2	2
Other types of investment	7571	2	1
Total	**476,611**	**100**	**134**

Source: *Malaysian Venture Capital and Private Equity Directory* 2009.

In 2008 the expansion/growth stage is still within the investment appetite of venture capital and private equity in Malaysia. The early stage shows a promising figure of RM82,785 million which can promote Islamic venture capital to a larger scale. Bridge, mezzanine, and pre-IPO amounted to RM60,366 million, which is also a healthy sign that private equity is gaining momentum in the industry. These figures show that Malaysia is attractive for Islamic venture capital and *Shari'ah* compliant private equity investments or companies.

According to the Gulf Venture Capital Association (GVCA), US$7.1 billion was raised in private equity funds in 2006 in the Middle East region. It was estimated in 2006 that Islamic private equity in the GCC region would be worth US$41 billion by 2011.[8] According to a research note provided by Tadhamon Capital on private equity in the MENA region, dated April 2011, as at 2010 private equity deals or transactions in the MENA region were stated to be worth US$1.07 billion.[9] Paul McNamara provides the following examples of funds established in the GCC:

- Enmaa (Dubai Growth Fund) from 3i Capital Group – US$100 million
- Indian Private Equity Fund from Khaleej Finance and Investment of Bahrain – US$200 million (invest [sic] in 50/50 in private equity and real estate in India)
- Al Imtiaz Investment Fund from Al Imtiaz Investment Company – Dinar denominated open ended private equity fund (focus on private equity and real estate)
- Global DIB Millenium Islamic Buyout Fund – US$500 million (focus on companies located in the GCC, Turkey, Egypt, Jordan, Lebanon, Tunisia and Morocco)
- Dhow Gulf Opportunities Fund launched by Qatar Islamic Bank – US$1 billion (focus on telecoms, environmental recycling technologies, media, oil and gas, and infrastructure)
- Rasmala MENA Private Equity Fund 2 by Rasmala from Dubai – US$350 million (*Shari'ah* compliant regional private equity fund target [sic] opportunities in Saudi Arabia, UAE and Egypt and mid-cap opportunities with an enterprise value of US$50 million to US$250 million)
- CMH Enterprise Fund I from Bahraini Bank CapitalManagement House – US$150 million (*Shari'ah* compliant private equity fund to invest in manufacturing, utility, energy, healthcare, services and technology related companies)
- DIC launched a fund with First Eastern Investment Group – US$1 billion (to target Chinese companies that want to expand in the Middle East)[10]

Foreign direct investment in 2006 in the MENA region was US$50 billion, which shows an inflow of investments due to economic growth.[11] This gives an advantage to the

MENA region in terms of developing the private equity market to assist in establishing favourable industries in the region to increase wealth and most importantly to widen the job market. The population continues to increase and if the government does not create a dynamic employment market it will leave many graduates unemployed. One of the best strategies for dealing with this is through business innovation and entrepreneurship through SMEs and private equity financing. In addition, the 2007 World Trade Organization (WTO) highlighted that the UAE's share in global trade increased by US$41 billion to US$275 billion in 2007, placing the country among the global top 30.[12]

High oil prices increased liquidity in the Middle East, which meant more opportunities for private equity. Family businesses play an important role in the economy of Saudi Arabia. Bridging family business and private equity can spur growth in private equity deals and bring the economy in the region to another level, creating a more dynamic employment market. Based on the funds presented and a brief analysis of the factors that can channel growth to private equity in the MENA region, it is of no doubt that the MENA region has the infrastructure for Islamic private equity investments.

Where Islamic private equity is concerned, structuring Islamic leveraged buyout has prospects in the Middle East. Private equity firms in the Middle East have demonstrated successful performance and made large profits. According to Usman Ahmed of Citi Islamic Banking in Dubai, there is a 'real demand for financing structures that look beyond the obvious senior unsecured debt equivalent' and 'need to be able to push down some of the financing to the level of the assets for which they are being raised'.[13] According to Qudeer Latif, Head of Islamic Finance (Middle East), law firm Clifford Chance advised Abraaj Capital's US$1.41

billion Islamic leveraged buyout acquisition of Egyptian Fertilizers Company in 2007.[14]

Venture capital is another potentially lucrative area of financing. As seen at the start of this chapter, Malaysia, supported by the government, is putting its utmost effort into developing the venture capital industry with funds mostly invested at the early stage and expansion and growth stage. The funds are smaller compared to those of private equity funds in the Middle East region. In 2008 Malaysia also introduced its first Islamic venture capital fund of RM35 million, managed by Musharaka Venture Management. However in the MENA region, venture capital is not as common as private equity deals. Based on the GVCA 2007 report, venture capital funds remain unattractive in the MENA region.[15] According to Veronica L. John:

> As the financial sectors and the economies in the emerging markets continue to develop, so will the PE [private equity] industries in those markets. The 1997–8 Asian crisis coupled with inherent political and economic risks, information asymmetry, financial markets volatility, serious corporate governance transparency concerns, and government corruption creates an environment ripe for skilled PE fund managers and investors to generate above average returns for their investors.[16]

According to this, challenges faced by countries in the emerging economy motivate the industry to improve because stable economic growth makes it attractive for foreign investments and thus expands the private equity and venture capital industry.

In the case of Vietnam, the Japanese government has shown a major interest in private equity investment. According to Dean Page and Brandon Boyle, '2010 has already seen a plethora of foreign firms raising funds for investments in Vietnam, and preliminary figures indicate that M&A [mergers and acquisitions] deal valuations have doubled in the first half of 2010 to over US$580 million.'[17] They also state:

> Several factors that contributed to Japan's interest in the private equity and the M&A market in Vietnam are due to operational synergies with Vietnamese firms which makes Vietnamese firms a particularly attractive destination for private equity investments. Japanese funds are clamoring to pair their Vietnamese investments with Japanese technology in sectors including automobile technology, information technology services, construction, transportation and finance.[18]

This is a brilliant evaluation of the Vietnamese private equity industry and definitely a win–win investment for both countries in terms of capital return and economic growth. It is a smart partnership between Japan and Vietnam and this can be a good example for countries which have already slowly developed the *Shari'ah* compliant private equity and Islamic venture capital industry, such as Malaysia and the GCC countries.

Southeast Asia in general has many opportunities for private equity financing. The economy is not affected on a large scale by the slowdown of the USA and Western Europe economies. Gustavo Eibin notes some key trends that make Southeast Asia attractive for private equity investing:

- a diversified region with a young, rapidly growing population fueling domestic consumption
- a region with a long-established commitment to market-based economies
- the beneficial impact of the Asian financial crisis (1997). The region has exhibited steady economic growth since

the crisis, mainly supported by the stabilisation of public finance
- the positive effects of globalisation
- relative immunity to the recent financial crisis and economic downturn along with strong growth outlook for the region
- small and mid-market opportunities[19]

This clearly shows that there are opportunities for innovation, research and development. The market and the industry are fresh with ideas, and partnership with foreign companies through private equity investments is a brilliant method to help create economic growth.

China also shows strong performance and development in the private equity and venture capital industry. There are opportunities in the agriculture, healthcare and media sectors, although the highest investment is in the manufacturing and services industry.[20] According to Seth Mallamo, writing in 2010:

> China's consumers have decided to spend much of their new found wealth on an improved diet with food expenditures growing 40% from 2004 to 2010. This trend is expected to continue with projected sales growing from 3.5 trillion RMB in 2010 to 4.7 trillion in 2015, for an increase of 34% during the period.[21]

He also states: 'Recent transactions include two by domestic fund Jiuding Capital, with a 110 million RMB investment in April of a Shanxi based pharmaceutical company, and a 34 million RMB investment a month earlier in medical researcher Qili Pharmaceutical.'[22]

The brief analysis above highlights those factors that play a key role in the performance of the private equity and venture capital industry. Although the regulatory system of a specific country may not converge with Islamic law, this will always be a small obstacle when compared to a private equity and venture capital industry that is underdeveloped. Nevertheless the economic growth of the emerging economy and the Middle East is happening at a good pace. The investment climate is fairly stable and not politically risky. Developed countries have definitely shown an interest in investing in South East Asia since, due to market opportunities, it is at the intermediate stage. This means that there is also an opportunity for *Shari'ah* compliant private equity funding and Islamic venture capital funding.

2.2 Small and medium-sized enterprises

Small and medium-sized enterprises have increasingly become a priority for policymakers in the Middle East and North Africa region, who see SMEs as key to improving competitiveness, raising incomes and generating employment. This section focuses on examples from the Middle East and Malaysia, due to their pioneering position in the *Shari'ah* compliant private equity and Islamic venture capital industry.

SMEs play a significant role in Malaysia's economic growth. SMEs may provide opportunities for break-throughs in innovation and new concepts for any product or service. The government has put a lot of effort into developing SMEs. In June 2004 the National SME Development Council was established to coordinate inter-ministry and -agency efforts in developing SMEs. The task of the ministries and agencies is to provide a policy-strategic framework for the industry's future.

'In November 2011 National SME Development Council

(NSDC) in Malaysia which is the highest policy making authority on Small and Medium Enterprise (SME) development endorsed the second phase of the SME Masterplan for the year 2012 to 2020.'[23] The first phase was endorsed in April 2011:

> The SME Masterplan is divided into two phases with the entire project to be completed in the third quarter of 2011. The Council deliberated on the First Phase of the Plan comprising a new SME Development Framework as well as broad policies and strategies to achieve the New Economic Model (NEM) goals. The Second Phase of the Masterplan will be undertaken to look into the specific action plans and the monitoring mechanism.[24]

The strategies for SME development as put forward by the National SME Development Council are:

- strengthening the infrastructure for SME development
- building the capacity of domestic SMEs
- enhancing access to financing for SMEs

Other than this, the Malaysian government has provided a comprehensive set of programmes through the various ministries and agencies, broadly categorised as 'financial assistance' and 'business support services'.[25] The financial assistance is broken down into several categories:[26]

- soft loans
- grants
- equity financing
- venture capital
- guarantee schemes
- tax incentives

The financial assistance and the business services offered by the government improve opportunities for venture capitalist financing. Venture capital is categorised as private sector funding. The venture capitalists are willing to take a stake in a business where they will provide capital, usually in exchange for a minority stake in the invested company. Businesses with a potential for being listed on the stock exchange are favoured targets for venture capitalists. The money is often provided for long-term expansion projects. This gives room for new funds or financial structures to fund companies at the start-up stage or at the later stage. If the financial structure to fund new companies provides a good return and adds value to the company in terms of management, transparency and corporate governance, it may be of demand in the market. Given that the SME industry in Malaysia is slowly moving upward, there is no doubt that the market is there to be taken advantage of.

Initially the National SME Development Council approved a comprehensive micro-finance institutional framework to promote the development of a sustainable micro-finance industry in Malaysia. The development of a sustainable and commercially driven micro-finance industry is important to ensure that micro-enterprises have adequate and continuous access to financing. The comprehensive micro-finance institutional framework is important as 80 per cent of SMEs in 2009 were micro-enterprises.

The micro-finance industry plays a major role in terms of financing for SMEs. However banks do not provide management advice to these new businesses. Although most businesses must give a comprehensive proposal as part of the loan application, management value added provided by the venture capital financing can be a useful tool for the entrepreneur of the new company. Their ownership may be at stake but that is negotiable in the venture capital industry.

This gives room for improvement in structuring new funds and improves existing funds that will give returns for both the financier and the entrepreneur.

The use of Islamic venture capital and *Shariʿah* compliant private equity in the venture capital industry is not as widespread as that of conventional methods of financing. The market for *Shariʿah* compliant funds already exists; improvisation is required in terms of efficiency of the processes, the convergence of tax legislation, innovation in business, fresh business ideas by the entrepreneurs, the search for human resources and the value creation of the investment.

2.3 Sectors invested in by private equity venture capital companies

According to the 2008 Deloitte report *Hidden Treasures: Private Equity Business in ASEAN*, the three key sectors that will attract the majority of private equity investments in the ASEAN region are manufacturing, financial services and consumer businesses.[27] The importance of the manufacturing sector was demonstrated when the industrial master plan (IMP) was formulated to further develop the manufacturing sector in Malaysia from 2001 to 2003. Tables 2.5 and 2.6 show Malaysian government investment by sector.

Table 2.5 *Malaysian government venture capital investment by sector (2001–3)*

Share of investment by sector (%)	2001	2002	2003
Manufacturing	43.7	40.9	34.7
ICT	17.0	19.4	37.1
Life sciences, medical, healthcare, biotechnology, etc.	4.8	7.7	16.8
Others	34.4	32.0	11.4
Total	**100.0**	**100.0**	**100.0**

Source: Bank Negara Malaysia Annual Report 2004.

Table 2.6 *Malaysian government venture capital investment by sector (2004–5)*

Sector	As at end 2004		As at end 2005	
	RM mil	% share	RM 000	% share
Information and communications technology	446.2	42.2	661,189.2	45.9
Manufacturing	269.2	25.4	292,906.2	20.3
Life sciences	194.7	18.4	270,574.1	18.8
Education	38.4	3.6	59,325.0	4.1
Electricity, power generation, gas and water	17.4	1.6	4,740.0	0.3
Wholesale, retail trade, restaurant and hotels	10.3	1.0	12,024.0	0.8
Financing, insurance, real estate and business services	6.8	0.6	15,963.2	1.1
Construction	0.1	0.0	100	0.0
Transport, storage and communications	0.0	0.0	15,970.0	1.1
Others	74.9	7.1	108,748.4	7.5
Total	**1058.1**	**100.0**	**1,441,540.2**	**100.0**

Source: Bank Negara Malaysia Annual Report 2004 and 2005.

It is clear that during these periods, the manufacturing and information technology sectors received high levels of investment from the government and also by venture capital companies. Since the inception of the multimedia super corridor, the ICT industry has boomed in Malaysia. By 2003, investments in ICT surpassed those in the manufacturing sector by approximately 3 per cent, the ICT industry remaining the leader in receiving venture capital funding. In 2005 the percentage of funding in the ICT sector rose to

45.9 per cent. The role of the venture capitalist in this sector can further boost growth and this is highlighted in some of the Malaysian government's policies, providing the supporting infrastructure and encouraging the development of technology and knowledge-based enterprises. The life sciences, medicine, healthcare and biotechnology industries are slowly gaining importance and with Malaysia's aim of becoming the world's leading hub for *halal* food, the biotechnology area in particular plays a significant role.

Table 2.7 *Malaysian government venture capital investment by sector (2007–8)*

Share of investment by sector (%)	2007	2008
Manufacturing	12.3	27.4
IT and communication	15.2	18.5
Life sciences	25.9	18
Others (education, transportation, electricity and power generation, transport, storage and communication)	46.6	36.1

Source: *Malaysian Venture Capital and Private Equity Directory 2009.*

The shift of investments from manufacturing to information technology and communication shows a healthy venture capital industry in terms of ideas, innovation and portfolio diversification. In 2007 and 2008, education, transportation, electricity and power generation, transport, storage and communication were the main attractions in the venture capital industry in Malaysia. Since 2008, manufacturing, IT and communication, and life sciences remain on the list of venture capital investments.

In the Middle East the US$1.5 billion Bahrain-based Islamic Development Bank Infrastructure Fund targets telecommunications, transportation, energy, natural resources, petrochemicals, water and other infrastructure sectors in

Muslim countries.[28] According to the Private Equity and Venture Capital Annual Report 2007, in the Middle East, basic materials in 2007 accounted for 23 per cent of the overall investment, the highest in the region.[29] The MENA region has also widened its private equity industry to diversify its investments and is slowly moving away from real estate investments. This is crucial in order to remain competitive and to attract international investors.

Table 2.8 *Venture capital investment by sector in the MENA region (2007)*

Share of investment by sector (%)	2007
Basic materials	23
Construction	7
Consumer goods	7
Financial services	16
Healthcare	9
Oil and gas	10
Transport	11
Others	17

Source: Private Equity and Venture Capital in the Middle East 2007 Annual Report.

Most sectors are related to infrastructure, which showed signs of growth. One of the biggest investments in 2007 was in the Egyptian Fertilizers Company, worth US$.4 billion. This comes under the 'basic materials' category.

2.4 Sources of venture capital in the MENA and ASEAN regions

In the MENA region the rise in oil prices has benefited many areas, including sovereign wealth funds (SWFs), the main source of private equity development. According to the *Private Equity and Venture Capital in the Middle East 2007 Annual Report*:

> SWF investment activity in the region has significantly increased in the last three years with 2007 having the largest number of investments. On the back of rising oil prices, funds have been accumulating reserves and MENA sovereign investment funds have become prominent players in the global market.

Figure 2.1 illustrates the sources of venture capital in Malaysia in 2004. The majority of funds come from the government and are given to venture capital companies and venture capital management companies in Malaysia. This is due to the small venture capital industry in Malaysia. Strong support by the government helps to boost the industry in the future. The second highest source of funding comes from corporations and the third highest from the banks. Lastly, Malaysia also has angel investors, but the numbers are small.

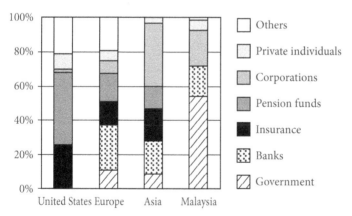

Figure 2.1 *Sources of venture capital in Malaysia (2004) compared to the US, Asian and European economies.*
Source: *Chok Kwee Bee, 'Collaboration with the Venture Capital Industry', presented at the Association Of Merchant Banks Tea Talk, April 2004.*

Venture capital companies in Malaysia are mostly corporate and not partnership structures such as private limited partnerships in the United States. As shown in Figure 2.1, in the United States the two main sources of funding for venture capital come from pension funds and insurance. In Europe, banks and pension funds are the main sources of funding for venture capital companies. In Asia, corporations, banks and insurance are the major sources of funds for the venture capital industry.

2.5 Venture capital contribution to the economy and employment in the MENA and ASEAN regions

The venture capital industry has contributed positively to the economy of most developed countries, particularly the United States and the United Kingdom. This section looks at the impact of venture capital not only from the point of view of a developed country, but also from the perspective of countries classed as emerging markets, such as Malaysia. The areas nurtured and developed by the venture capital industry include information technology, biotechnology, manufacturing and education.

The spirit of entrepreneurship has also managed to promote employment and increase research and development (R&D) for new concepts and products. The venture capital business has encouraged R&D in most of the sectors present in a particular country. In the USA, research and development is in excess of billions of US dollars. Global Insight found that ventured firms, adjusted for size, spend over twice as much on research and development as non-ventured firms.[30] According to Global Insight, even when small ventured firms grow to be among the biggest in their industry, they remain leaders in research and development.

Global Insight also found that that many of the ventured

companies founded during venture capital's infancy have quickly grown from small private companies to some of the largest in the USA. It also stated that of the top firms in the USA for research and development spending, many are either ventured themselves, such as Microsoft, Cisco and Intel, or were major acquirers of ventured firms, like Johnson & Johnson and Pitzer.

Malaysia aspires to be a biotechnology hub and launched the National Biotechnology Policy on 28 April 2005 to create employment and contribute to the country's GDP. The policy is divided into three main phases: Phase I (2005–10), Phase II (2010–15) and Phase III (2016–20). The policy aims to build a conducive environment for R&D and industry development while leveraging on the country's existing areas of strength.[31]

This clearly shows that Malaysia is focusing on investments in the area of research and development. In the venture capital business, biotechnology has made its way into the venture capitalists' portfolio. This comes under the life-science area where in 2005 it comprised RM194.7 million of the overall venture capital investment. The information and communications technology sector was the highest in 2005, with RM446.2 million invested by venture capitalists. These figures indicate that research and development plays a vital role as new products and concepts are nurtured in this sector.[32] According to Zarinah Anwar, writing in 2006:

The growth of the venture capital industry in Malaysia has been on a positive track. As at end 2005, the number of committed funds has risen to RM2.6 billion from RM2.1 billion in 2003. The number of investee companies has also grown by 30 percent since 2003. Statistics also show that the private sector is fast taking over the role of government as the prime source for these funds. It has become more apparent that we are now experiencing a strong acceptance of venture capital, as an alternative vehicle into the mainstream capital market products of debt, equity and derivative instruments.'[33]

According to the 2002 Survey of the Economic and Social Impact of Venture Capital in Europe compiled by the European Venture Capital Association, the companies surveyed in Europe used venture capital funding to achieve significant increases in their budgets for research and development, marketing and training. The survey also highlighted that, for all companies, the initial venture capital investment was followed by a sharp increase in spending for research and development. Half the seed/start-up companies multiplied their efforts in this area by more than four times, while half the expansion stage companies almost doubled the amount invested. Based on the survey, most of the investment in seed/start-up and expansion focused on computer-related technology/products, communications and biotechnology.

In 2003 China rose to third in the world in terms of the money it spent on research and development. According to a 2003 report by the Organisation for Economic Co-operation and Development (OECD), China's expenditure in research and development reached USD60 billion in 2001, behind only the United States and Japan whose investment was respectively 282 billion and 104 billion dollars respectively, according to the Beijing-based *Economic Daily*.[34]

This shows that venture capital plays a vital role in research and development in many sectors, in particular the technology, communications and biotechnology sectors. This is yesterday's news for the US and Europe (the UK holds the largest venture capital industry) but Malaysia's economy depends on new ideas and innovation to increase the growth of its economy and increase foreign investments.

It is obvious that all developed nations are spending large sums on research and development to sustain their market share and economy in the world. The impact of this is clear in developed countries such as the US and UK, which means that with the right economic planning and infrastructure, the same can be true in an emerging market such as Malaysia.

The venture capital industry in Malaysia may be small but the number of invested companies rose tremendously during 2009–11. The total sum of money invested overall has reached billions (ringgit). This is a healthy sign for the nation's economy because product innovation in the market helps to keep the economy stable, particularly if they are in demand in the market and are profitable. Furthermore, new companies established through venture capital funding help to create jobs in the industries that the venture capitalists invest in.

According to Global Insight, in the United States the venture capital contribution to jobs employed more than 10 million American workers and generated US$1.8 trillion in sales in 2003.[35] Based on the statistics obtained from Global Insight, invested companies in biotechnology posted an employment gain of 23 per cent and healthcare products grew by 16 per cent between 2000 and 2003.

According to Global Insight, ventured firms grow faster

Table 2.9 *Company and employment (US)*

Company	Employment
Seagate	10,000
Google	1,600
eBay	6,200
The Home Depot	299,000

Source: Venture Impact 2004.[36]

than their national industry counterparts but sectors with a higher concentration of venture capital financing experienced higher employment growth differentials.[37] The best example is the computer software industry, where venture-backed firms in 2003 employed 88 per cent of all computer software workers and venture-backed firms grew by 17 per cent, while the industry as a whole declined by nearly 8 per cent. [38] Table 2.9 shows employment figures at selected venture-backed firms in 2003.[39] In the case of Malaysia where the venture capital industry is small, it does not stop the job-creation process. It does not surpass the overall employment rate, but in the future, as investment by venture capitalists increases, it can build up to a good percentage.

2.6 Conclusion

The development of SMEs can also create opportunities for the development of *Shari'ah* compliant private equity and Islamic venture capital. Furthermore, it can add to the list of choices that may be used by the entrepreneur when starting up a business. The entrepreneur may choose to opt with partnership through profit-sharing or pay interest to lenders. Statistics have shown that government support in countries in the Middle East and Malaysia has pushed the industry to a higher level. Sources of funds to promote *Shari'ah* compliant private equity and the Islamic venture capital industry in the respective countries are also in abundance.

In the remaining chapters, the features of *Shari'ah* compliant private equity and Islamic venture capital funding are discussed in detail in terms of the benefits of profit-sharing applied in private equity and venture capital, the entrepreneurs', management's and investors' rights and responsibilities, valuation methods, exit strategies, and monitoring methods.

Notes

1. Deloitte, *Hidden Treasures: Private Equity Business in ASEAN,* p. 1, http://www.deloitte.com/assets/Dcom-Global / Local%20Assets/Documents/gfsi_Hidden Treasures Private Equity Business in ASEAN_July2008.pdf (retrieved 2 February 2011).

2. Ibid.

3. 'Singapore's CMI capital launches $US2million private equity fund', *Singapore Business News,* 8 September 2011, http:// singaporebusiness.asia/singapore%E2%80%99s-cmia-capital-launches-us200m-private-equity-fund (retrieved 8 September 2011).

4. Bank Negara Malaysia Annual Report (2004), p. 194, http:// www.bnm.gov.my/files/publication/ar/en/2004/ar2004. complete.pdf (retrieved 5 September 2010).

5. Ibid. p. 194.

6. Ibid.

7. Ibid. p. 195.

8. Catharina Sophie Bescht, 'Islamic private equity outgrowing conventional private equity', *Islamic Finance News,* October 2007.

9. Junaid Jafar and Osman Mian, Tad Lamon Capital Research Note: *Private Equity in the MENA Region,* April 2011, p. 1.

10. Paul McNamara, 'Islamic investment banking 2009', Yassar Media, p. 15.

11. Zeinab Karake-Shalhoub, 'Private equity, Islamic finance and sovereign wealth funds in the MENA Region', *Thunderbird International Business Review,* 2008, vol. 50, no. 6, p. 360.

12. Ibid.

13. 'Asia on the lookout for Islamic LBOs', *Asiamoney,* April 2008, p. 19.

14. Ibid.

15. GVCA and KPMG, *Private Equity and Venture Capital in the Middle East 2007, Annual Report 2008,* p. 53, http://www.

kpmg.es/docs/PrivateEqVenture.pdf (retrieved 5 February 2012).

16. Veronica L. John, 'Opportunities for private equity in emerging markets', *Thunderbird School of Global Management Quarterly*, 2010, http://www.thunderbird.edu/knowledge_ network/ctrs_excellence/tgpec/newsletter/articles/oppor tunities_for_private_emerging.htm (retrieved 5 September 2011).

17. Dean Page and Brandon Boyle, 'Japanese eye expansion of private equity investment in Vietnam', *Thunderbird School of Global Management Quarterly,* 2010, http://www.thunder bird.edu/knowledge_network/ctrs_excellence/tgpec/newslet ter/articles/_japanese_interest_in_vietnam.htm (retrieved 5 September 2011).

18. Ibid.

19. Gustavo Eibin, 'Southeast Asia: Maximising returns through global partnerships', *Thunderbird School of Global Management Quarterly*, 2010, http://www.thunderbird.edu/ knowledge_network/ctrs_excellence/tgpec/newsletter/arti cles/_southeast_asia.htm (retrieved 5 September 2011).

20. Seth Mallamo (2010), 'Seeking growth: opportunities for private equity in China', *Thunderbird School of Global Management Quarterly*, 2010, http://www.thunderbird.edu/ knowledge_network/ctrs_excellence/tgpec/newsletter/arti cles/_opportunities_pe_china.htm (retrieved 5 September 2011).

21. Ibid.

22. Ibid.

23. SME Info: One Stop SME Resources, 'SME masterplan to accelerate growth of SMEs through comprehensive actions including six high impact programmes', 23 November 2011, http://www.smeinfo.com.my/index.php/en/component/ content/article/162-top-news/1348-sme-masterplan-to- accelerate-growth-of-smes-through-comprehensive-actions-

including-six-high-impact-programmes (retrieved 9 May 2012).

24. SME Corp. Malaysia Official Website, 'SME masterplan for innovation-led and productivity-driven growth to achieve high income nation', http://www.smecorp.gov.my/v4/node/76 (retrieved 9 May 2012).

25. SME Info: One Stop Resources, Business Support Services, http://www.smeinfo.com.my/index.php?option=com_content&view=article&id=121&Itemid=80&lang=en (retrieved 14 January 2010).

26. SME Info: One Stop Resources, Financial Assistance, http://www.smeinfo.com.my/index.php?option=com_content&view=article&id=143&Itemid=65&lang=en (retrieved 14 January 2010).

27. Deloitte, *Hidden Treasures: Private Equity Business in ASEAN*, p. 10, http://www.deloitte.com/assets/Dcom-Global/Local%20Assets/Documents/gfsi_HiddenTreasuresPrivate EquityBusinessinASEAN_July2008.pdf (retrieved 2 February 2011).

28. Business Wire, 6 October 1998. Islamic Development Bank Launches US$1.5 Billion Infrastructure Fund, http://www.thefreelibrary.com/Islamic+Development +Bank+Launches+US$1.5Billion+Infrastructure+Fund. -a053063029 (retrieved 2 February 2011).

29. GVCA and KPMG, *Private Equity and Venture Capital in the Middle East 2007, Annual Report 2008*, p. 53.

30. Global Insight, *Venture Impact 2004: Venture Capital Benefits to the US Economy*, http://www.cnel.gov.pt/document/venture_impact_2004.pdf, p. 11 (retrieved 20 February 2011).

31. Malaysian Biotechnology Information Centre, National Biotechnology Policy, http://www.bic.org.my/?action=local scenario&do=policy (retrieved 9 May 2012).

32. Bank Negara Malaysia Annual Report (2004), p. 195.

33. Zarinah Anwar, introductory speech to the Venture Capital Investors Forum 2006, 21 August 2006, http://www.sc.com.my/eng/html/resources/speech/sp_20060821.html (retrieved 10 January 2011).

34. 'China rises to third in research, development spending', *China Daily*, 3 November 2003, http://www.chinadaily.com.cn/en/doc/2003-11/03/content_277867.htm (retrieved 24 February 2010).

35. Global Insight, *Venture Impact 2004: Venture Capital Benefits to the US Economy*.

36. Ibid. p. 4.

37. Ibid.

38. Ibid.

39. Ibid.

CHAPTER 3

SCOPE OF *SHARI'AH* BASED COMPLIANT PRIVATE EQUITY AND ISLAMIC VENTURE CAPITAL

This chapter discusses the financial advantages and product development of *Shari'ah* based and *Shari'ah* compliant partnership financing. These modes of financing (*shirkah*, *mushārakah* and *mudhārabah*) are based on partnership and adhere to *Shari'ah* law. *Shari'ah* based modes of financing do not need to undergo processes to make them *Shari'ah* compliant. *Shari'ah* compliant private equity and Islamic venture capital, on the other hand, are structured to ensure there are no interest charges or investments involving products and services that are forbidden according to *Shari'ah* law.

A *Shari'ah* compliant private equity fund is a financing vehicle that abides by the principles of *Shari'ah* law. It can be based on a *Shari'ah* structure and adhere to the profit- and loss-sharing principles of *shirkah* (partnership), notably *mushārakah* and *mudhārabah*. *Mushārakah* profits and losses are divided among the shareholders depending on how much capital each has invested. *Mudhārabah* profits are shared between the investors and the fund managers as *mudarib* but losses are borne entirely by the investors. A *Shari'ah* compliant private equity fund can only invest in companies which are engaged in *halal* activities and comply with financial screens similar to those used for stock selection by the Dow Jones Islamic indices for public equity. Some *Shari'ah* compliant private equity funds are structured conventionally with general and limited partners but compliance is achieved simply through screening.

Islamic venture capital can be provided through a private equity fund but this only occurs in the early stages of the business. *Shari'ah* requirements are similar to those relating to *Shari'ah* private equity funds; for example the investment has to be in *halal* activities and companies with excessive leverage are excluded.

Later in the chapter discussion turns to the structure of *shirkah* and *mushārakah* (both *Shari'ah* based) and their features and concepts in Islamic law. *Mushārakah* is chosen for discussion as it entails a financial structure based on venture capital and allows discussion of the scope of a *Shari'ah* based product. The chapter concludes with a section on how *mushārakah* applies to the venture capital and private equity industry.

3.1 Definition of '*Shari'ah* compliant' from the perspective of private equity and venture capital

3.1.1 Abolition of interest

It is vital that any Islamic financial contract and funding are free from *riba*. This is an important element that ensures the *Shari'ah* compliancy of any Islamic financial contract. The abolition and forbiddance of *riba*, or interest, has been stated in the Al-Quran on several occasions. For example:

> Those who swallow usury cannot rise up save as he ariseth whom the devil hath prostrated by (his) touch. That is because they say: Trade is just like usury; whereas Allah permitteth

trading and forbiddeth usury. He unto whom an admonition from his Lord cometh, and (he) refraineth (in obedience thereto), he shall keep (the profits of) that which is past, and his affair (henceforth) is with Allah. As for him who returneth (to usury) – Such are rightful owners of the fire. They will abide therein. (Al Quran. Al-Baqarah 2: 275)

The definition of interest (the literal meaning of interest, or *al-riba* as it is used in the Arabic language) is 'increase'. *Riba* has been described as a loan with the condition that the borrower will pay more than the amount borrowed. In other words *riba* or interest is the cost of borrowed money.

Riba (usury) is of two major kinds, *riba al-buyu'i* and *riba al-qardhi*. *Riba al-buyu'i* is the type of *riba* that occurs on the exchange of goods and involves payments. This *riba* is divided into three categories:

- **Riba al-fadhli**. The selling of *ribawi* items whereby the excess is taken via the exchange of specific homogenous items and through hand-to-hand purchase. An example would be exchanging dates of superior quality in a certain amount for dates of inferior quality in a greater amount. The addition in this transaction is considered as *riba* and it is *haram*. This is stated in a *hadith* by Prophet Muhammad (saw):

Abu Sa'id al-Khudri (Allah be pleased with him) reported, Allah's Messenger (may peace be upon him) as saying: Gold is to be paid for by gold, silver by silver, wheat by wheat, barley by barley, dates by dates, salt by salt, like by like, payment being made hand to hand. He who made an addition to it, or asked for an addition, in fact dealt in usury. The receiver and the giver are equally guilty. (Sahih Muslim. 10: 3854)

- **Riba al-yad.** The selling or exchange of different *ribawi* items in cash where either one of the goods is delivered later.
- **Riba al-nasi'ah.** The selling of different *ribawi* items on deferred terms. When the goods arrive and the seller cannot pay for them, the tenure is added together with the addition in payment.

Riba al-qardhi is a contract on debt or loan for a specified tenure and additional payment on the debt or the loan. This is similar to that of the interest practised in conventional banks. In the case of private equity funding, leverage is used at the consolidation stage where private equity companies use debt to buy out the company. This is a leveraged buyout (LBO). However, there is an LBO that is *Shari'ah* compliant whereby only 33.3 per cent of debt is used.

3.1.2 Industries permissible according to Islamic law
To ensure that an Islamic banking and finance contract is *Shari'ah* compliant, any businesses it invests in must be *halal* according to Islamic law. *Halal* in this situation means potential investments in small business companies related to products and services that are permissible in Islam such as information technology, tourism and hospitality, healthcare and others. Businesses involved in gambling, pornography, speculating and liquor are examples of businesses that are not permissible in Islam.

3.1.3 Types of partnership and company structure in Islamic law
This section looks at studies on *shirkah* and *mushārakah* by three authors, Muhammad Taqi Usmani, Ibn-Taimiyah and Engku Rabiah Adawiah, to help gain a better understanding of the terms, categories, features and operations

of *shirkah* and *mushārakah*. Muhammad Taqi Usmani states that authors who have written on Islamic banking and finance introduced the term *mushārakah* (partnership), and it is normally restricted to a particular type of *shirkah* (partnership), which is the *shirkat-ul-amwal*.[1] *Shirkah* can be divided into two categories, *shirkah ul-milk* and *shirkah-ul-'aqd*.

Shirkah ul-milk is a joint ownership between two or more partners in a particular property. However, according to Muhamad Taqi Usmani, this kind of *shirkah* may come into existence in two different ways. First, if two or more persons purchase equipment, it will be owned jointly by all of them and the relationship between them with regard to that property is called *shirkah ul-milk*.

> In this case, this relationship came into existence at their own option because they had elected to purchase the equipment jointly. However, there are cases where this kind of *shirkah* operates without any action taken by the parties. In the case of a death of a partner, all the latter's heirs inherit his or her property which comes into their joint ownership as an automatic consequence upon the death of the partner.[2]

The second type of *shirkah* is *shirkah-ul-'aqd*, meaning partnership in a business through a mutual contract. There are three kinds of *shirkah-ul-'aqd*:

- **Shirkat-ul-amwal**. Where all the partners invest some capital into a commercial enterprise or a business venture.
- **Shirkat-ul-a'mal**. Where all the partners jointly undertake to render some services for their customers and the fee charged to the customers is distributed among the partners to an agreed ratio. However, if the income

earned goes to a joint pool, it can be distributed between them irrespective of the work put in by each partner.

- **Shirkat-ul-wujooh.** For this type of shirkah the partners have no investment at all. They purchase the commodities at a deferred price and sell them on the spot. The profit earned is distributed between them at an agreed ratio.

The partnership transaction according to Ibn Taimiyah is divided into two categories: partnership in property (*shirkah al-amlak*) and partnership in contracts (*shirkah al-'uqud*).[3] The five forms of partnership in contracts mentioned by Ibn-Taimiyah are:

- **Partnership in capital and labour (*shirkah al-inan*).** Two or more persons pool their capital, work together and share in the profits.
- **Partnership in labour (*shirkah al-abdan*).** Artisans or labourers jointly undertake a task and agree to distribute their earnings amongst themselves.
- **Partnership in credit (*shirkah al-wujuh*).** One or more of the members procures goods on credit, sells them and distributes the profits.
- **Comprehensive partnership (*shirkah al-mufawadah*).** Partners combine in every type of *shirkah*, namely *al-inan*, *al-wujuh* and *al-abdan*.
- **Mudhārabah partnership (*shirkah al-mudhārabah*).** One party provides labour and the other party provides capital.

Engku Rabiah Adawiah states that liabilities remain the same under Islamic law up to the amount of their capital contribution and that there are no separate contracts on the basis of pure business structures, be it partnership or companies. She also states that paramount in determining liability in Islamic law is not the business structure, but the actual *shirkah* contracts between the parties. She adds that if the parties want limited liability, they can choose *shirkah al-inan* or *mudhārabah* and if they want unlimited liability, they can choose *shirkah al-mufawadah*.[4]

This shows that in a *mushārakah* the partners may choose and negotiate whether to opt for limited liability or unlimited liability. Furthermore in a *shirkah* and *mushārakah*, no partner is liable for the other partners' financial liability unless permission is given by the other partners on behalf of the partnership. Although any partner may become an agent for all other partners for all kinds of business transactions in the partnership (not outside), no partner is financially liable for the transactions that are made personally by other partners.[5]

Two business entities are present in the private equity and venture capital industry: the limited liability company and the limited partnership. Therefore it is not the business structure that determines liability in Islamic Law, rather the actual *shirkah* contracts between the parties. In this way there is a win–win situation for both parties. This is an advantage in applying *mushārakah* in the venture capital and private equity company whereby the flexibility of Islamic law gives partners the option to choose and negotiate on opting for a limited liability or unlimited liability contract. This paves the way for structuring a *Shari'ah* based contract whereby a financial contract is customised to close deals with benefits and advantages between investors and entrepreneurs.

3.2 Modes of Islamic financing for private equity and venture capital funding

This section looks at the advantages of those modes of financing that already exist in *Shari'ah* law over structuring an existing fund to make it *Shari'ah* compliant. *'Shari'ah* based' captures the essence of the spirit of Islam and this is reflected in the *shirkah* partnership type of financing, for example *mushārakah* and *mudhārabah*.

3.2.1 *Classic* mushārakah

Classic *mushārakah* is when two or more parties join capital in the form of cash or assets and the shares are distributed (equity participation) based on the capital contribution. *Mushārakah* is partnership based on profit and loss sharing. In the *mushārakah* financing contract, two or more parties contribute their capital as well as expertise in the joint venture or the partnership. Profit and loss are normally shared based on the capital contribution. This type of *mushārakah* becomes the basis of other sub-*mushārakah* products engineered in the 1990s such as diminishing *mushārakah*. The investors or the bank give the initial investment to the entrepreneur, both form a *mushārakah* partnership and the profit-sharing rate is determined.

For example, the partnership is between the entrepreneur and the bank. The entrepreneur takes a loan from the bank and engages in a *mushārakah* partnership. The loan given by the bank is the initial investment into the existing business set up by the entrepreneur. The bank and the entrepreneur then determine the profit ratio. The payments to the bank by the entrepreneur are based on this profit ratio. A *mushārakah* account is then set up by the bank to manage the loan given to the entrepreneur. The entrepreneur has to provide the bank with a financial report on the business as part of the monitoring process required by the bank.

To put this into perspective, in Indonesia, Bank Muamalat opened a pilot project where the Bandung

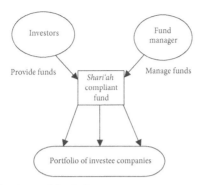

Figure 3.1 *Classic* mushārakah *structure*

branch was assigned to the implementation of *mudārabah* and *mushārakah* in the West Java province.[6] According to research based on this, short-term projects are preferred by small and medium-sized entrepreneurs as they do not want to take greater risks by involving themselves in long-term projects which may also cause liquidity problems. Other than this, working capitals for the short-term projects are provided by the bank on a profit-sharing basis and banks evaluate the project beforehand to set the profit-sharing ratio, taking into consideration the risks involved.[7] This research also looks at the bank's longer-term profit sharing which is by purchase of contract, with deferred payment on a monthly basis. The structure of this type of *mushārakah* in an Islamic venture capital or private equity setting is shown in Figure 3.1.

In Figure 3.1, the fund manager manages the funds and investments. The *Shariʻah* compliant fund holds the investment fund. Being an entrepreneur, the individuals and their team run the company and share in the profit and the losses with the investors and fund manager. The portfolio comprises a number of businesses taken in as investments by the fund manager.

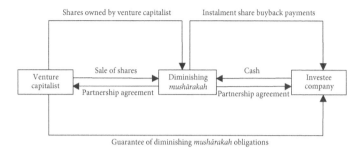

Figure 3.2 *Diminishing* mushārakah *structure*

3.2.2 *Diminishing* mushārakah

This type of *mushārakah* is a partnership contract that binds buyer and financier into an agreement whereby the buyer buys out his share from the other party until he (the buyer) fully owns the asset. The structure of this type of *mushārakah* is shown in Figure 3.2.

In Figure 3.2, the diminishing *mushārakah* is structured as a special purpose vehicle (SPV). Both the investee company and the venture capitalist enter into a partnership agreement and determine the profit ratio. The investee company will buy out its shares from the venture capitalist at an agreed price. Diminishing *mushārakah* as an exit strategy is further discussed in Chapter 6.

For a home loan, the diminishing *mushārakah* is applied as such. For example, buyer A takes up a loan from bank B. During the tenure of the loan the buyer charges rent to a tenant of the house and later on uses the rent to repay his loan. In the meantime the loan is slowly diminishing. Figure 3.3 shows how a home loan operates under diminishing *mushārakah*.

3.2.3 *Temporary* mushārakah

Temporary *mushārakah* is working capital finance. The bank invests on a short-term scale and receives its invested

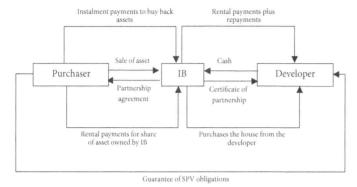

Figure 3.3 *Diminishing* mushārakah *structure for a home loan.*
(Source: Rodney Wilson, 2005)[8]

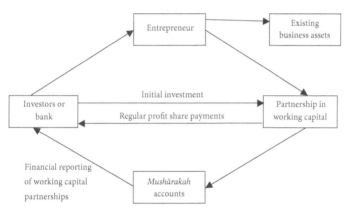

Figure 3.4 *Temporary* mushārakah *structure.*
(Source: Rodney Wilson, 2005)[9]

capital plus profit at the end of an agreed period. A temporary *mushārakah* can be renewed depending on the
agreement of the partners. The structure of the temporary
mushārakah (see Figure 3.4) is different to that of the permanent one in terms of the tenure of investment. In this
case the existing business is an established business, only
it needs funds to improve its performance. Furthermore,
working capital finance is needed to finance accounts

payable and wages. It is not used to finance a long-term investment as seen in the structure of the permanent *mushārakah*.

The temporary *mushārakah* may not necessarily be applicable for *Shari'ah* compliant private equity and Islamic venture capital because it is used for short-term funding. The three types of *mushārakah* discussed here indicate how *mushārakah* operates in the finance industry.

3.3 Concept and features of *mushārakah*

In this section the features of *mushārakah* are discussed, looking at management, ownership and profit, losses, risk, contract tenure and termination, financial advantages, and lastly limited liability. The concept of *mushārakah* is based on sharing. Sharing in these matters applies to managing the partnership or joint venture, profit, losses and risk. *Mushārakah* highlights *Shari'ah* approved business activities that are *halal* and can be supported in an Islamic economy.

3.3.1 *Management*

Mushārakah is a mode of financing that achieves a win–win situation for both capital providers and entrepreneurs who hold a stake in the company. According to Sami Al-Suwailem, Deputy Director of the Islamic Research and Training Institute of the Islamic Development Bank, from an Islamic point of view, venture capital is based on equity financing (*shirkah al-inan*) and thus falls within the framework of Islamic finance. He also emphasises that it combines economic viability, Islamic preferably, making it a promising option for Islamic financial institutions.[10] *Mushārakah* involves shared management among the business partners. Shared management is explained below in terms of partners' rights and responsibilities in the business and towards one another.

First, every partner is an agent to the other. Any work done by one partner is deemed to be authorised by other partners. If the partner purchases for themselves it will be at their own expense and not used for the business. The actual possession of a property from the *mushārakah* business is considered a possession of the other partners, as if a partner purchases a half portion of a specific item for themselves and a half portion for the *mushārakah*.[11] Second, every partner has the right to actively participate in the *mushārakah* business. There are occasions whereby the partners may agree upon a condition that the management shall be carried out by some partners while the others become sleeping partners. The sleeping partners in this case are entitled to the profit only to the extent of their own investment and the ratio of profit given to them should not exceed the ratio of the investment. Third, every partner enjoys equal rights in the *mushārakah*, although a partner is not to burden the other partners with debts.

3.3.2 Ownership

Ownership is a crucial element in venture capital investment. Chris Bovaird in his *Introduction to Venture Capital Finance* (1990) states that venture capital is equity based, more participatory and longer term for maturity and the participation required of the venture capital investor extends beyond mere provision of capital.[12] He explains that typically a venture capitalist will seek between 20 and 49.9 per cent of the common shares of the company and the size of the stake must be large enough to influence his fellow shareholders. He also states that the shares exchanged in return for the financial injection allow the venture capitalist to share in the company's profits, to exercise voting rights in matters relating to the company's management and strategy, and to exercise all of the other rights and privileges that a co-owner or partner might enjoy.

Venture capital in terms of ownership exhibits features similar to those of *mushārakah* financing. Both parties in this case enjoy similar rights, liabilities and share ownership and the venture capital firm has control over the business. The proportion of profit to be distributed must be agreed upon at the time of affecting the contract and it is distributed in proportions settled by the partners in advance and in proportion or percentage. The profit must be based on actual profit earned and not fixed, depending on the success and profitability of the business. However, in the case of a private equity, which consists of a more complex funding structure, it may be engineered with *mushārakah*-type contracts.

> The Shāfi'ī and Mālikī jurists are also in view that [*sic*] the profit will be distributed in proportion to the amounts of capital invested which means a fixed sum of money because profit cannot be completed for any party. According to Hanafī jurists profit shares must be given as a proportion of the profit and not in a fixed sum of money. The Hanafī and the Hanbalī jurists support this. As for the Shāfi'ī and Mālikī schools, the distribution of profit must reflect the proportion of invested capital.[13]

3.3.3 Losses

Losses in a *mushārakah* are distributed in proportion to the capital invested and borne by the owners of the capital. All schools of Islamic jurisprudence are in agreement on this.[14] Therefore if a partner has invested 70 per cent of the capital they must suffer 70 per cent of the losses. This is because losses result in the erosion of equity and capital. If the loss is incurred in one period it should be adjusted with the profit obtained in the following periods until all the losses are written off and the capital is restored to its original level.[15]

Any distribution of profit that occurs during that period of writing off the losses will be considered as an advance to the partners. In the case of a partner without capital the jurists state that they are not liable for the losses because they do not have capital and losses imply the erosion of capital. Therefore the losses will be answered by the partner with capital. However, they still bear the risk on the investment. This feature of the *mushārakah* only forces the partner (the investor in the case of a venture capital or the venture capital management company) with the highest capital to work in accordance with its capital and monitor the investments at all times.

Apart from this, information on the investment or any work carried out is disseminated accordingly because the profit in a *mushārakah* contract does not have to be shared in accordance to capital contributions, though this differs among all four schools of Islamic jurisprudence.

3.3.4 Forms of capital in mushārakah

According to Mufti Taqi Usmani in his *Introduction to Islamic Finance* (2005), most of the Muslim jurists are of the opinion that the capital invested by each partner must be in a liquid form such as cash and not in the form of commodities.[16] The four schools in Islamic jurisprudence have different perspectives on this issue.

Imam Malik states that liquidity of capital is not a condition for the validity of *mushārakah*. Commodities may be used and the partner contributes to the *mushārakah* partnerships. The share is determined on the basis of the evaluation of the market price at the time the contract takes place.

Imam Abu Hanifah and Imam Ahmad are of the opinion that such a contribution should not be accepted in *mushārakah*. This is due to reasons such as the ability to distinguish from one another the commodities contributed by each partner. For example, if one partner contributes a piece of land and the other partner contributes another piece of land, each piece of land is owned exclusively by each partner. If the land of one partner is sold, the proceeds should go to the owner of the piece of land and the other partner cannot share the profit as they have no right to claim a share of its price. In this situation, a partnership cannot take place because the capital is distinguishable one from the other and it cannot be pooled, as compared to monetary capital.

In the case of redistribution of share capital, if it is in the form of commodities the redistribution cannot take place because the commodities may have been sold at that time. If the capital is repaid on the basis of its value and it has increased, there is a possibility that a partner receives all the profit of the business due to the appreciation on the value of the commodity they invested in, while the other partner may receive nothing. 'If the value of the commodity decreases, there is a possibility that a partner can secure some part of the original price of the commodity of the other partner in addition to his own instrument.' [17]

Imam Al-Shafi'i states that commodities are of two types, *dhawat-ul-amthal* and *dhawat-ul-qeemah*. *Dhawat-ul-amthal* is a category of commodities which can be replaced by similar commodities in quality and quantity, such as wheat, rice and barley. *Dhawat-ul-qeemah* are commodities which cannot be replaced by similar commodities, such as sheep, lamb and cattle. Each head of sheep cannot be replaced with another sheep as it has its own characteristics not found in any other sheep. If a person kills the sheep, they are required to pay the price of the sheep to the owner and it is not replaced by a similar sheep.

According to Muhammad Taqi Usmani, Imam Al-Shafi'i says that the commodities of *dhawat-ul-amthal* may be contributed to the *mushārakah* as part of the share of capital. Yet commodities of *dhawat-ul-qeemah* may not form part of the share capital.[18] This second point as stated by Imam Ahmad and Imam Hanifah is already addressed by Imam Al-Shafi'i, in the sense that the partners can give similar commodities invested to each partner for redistribution of capital. Under the first point, however, Imam Abu Hanifah says that commodities under the category of *dhawat-ul-amthal* may form parts of share capital because they can be mixed together and become indistinguishable. If the commodity is from the category *dhawat-ul-qeemah* then it may not form parts of the share capital.

These differing views show that the types of capital may be both cash and commodity. In the case of the commodity, it has to be evaluated as per the market price at the time that the *mushārakah* contract takes place. The market value will determine the share capital of the partner.

3.3.5 *Termination of* mushārakah

Mushārakah can be terminated at any time and the particular partner has a right to do so. Normally contract tenure is on a long-term basis ranging from three to five years; however it depends on the companies involved. The distribution of assets of these partners upon the termination differs depending on the form of assets the company has. If the assets are in cash form, they will be distributed on a pro rata basis between the partners.[19] If not, however, the partners will decide on the liquidation or on the distribution of the assets (not in cash form) between them. In cases where the assets cannot be liquidated and distributed evenly, they will be sold off and the profits distributed among the partners.

If one partner dies, their share in the company will either be taken by their heirs or remain in the company depending on the heirs' decision. The deceased partner's contract will automatically be terminated but the contract can remain in the company and again depends on the heirs' decision. If any one of the partners becomes insane the partnership terminates automatically. There are situations where one partner terminates the contract and the business remains. If this happens, it can be settled through mutual agreement. The shares owned by the leaving partner are valued (determined through mutual consent) and distributed among the other partners who want to purchase them. If the partners do not come to an agreed price, the leaving partner can compel the other partners on the liquidation or the distribution of the assets themselves.[20]

However according to Mufti Taqi Usmani, there is another issue pertaining to this:

> The question arises whether the partners can agree, while entering into the contract of the Mushārakah, on a condition that the liquidation or separation of the business shall not be effected unless all the partners, or the majority of them wants to do so, and that a single partner who wants to come out of the partnership shall have to sell his share to the other partners and shall not force them on liquidation or separation. Most of the traditional books of Islamic Fiqh seem to be silent on this question. It appears that there is no bar from the Shari'ah point of view if the partners agree to such a condition right at the beginning of the Mushārakah. This is expressly permitted by some Hanbalī jurists.[21]

3.3.6 Limited liability

Limited liability is another feature of the *mushārakah*. Limited liability in this case is due to the limited losses and profit borne by the shareholders or the partners. They are not held liable for more than the amount they invested. This is as with the limited liability feature of a corporation. The requirement of the limited liability makes it necessary to regard *mushārakah* as an entity separate from the individuality of the shareholders.[22] This common *urf* results in a stable *mushārakah* as a financing tool for the shareholders and the parties involved. This is a benefit of the *mushārakah* and profit-sharing instruments. This feature of the *mushārakah* protects the shareholders and their investment, and therefore is a good tool in equity financing and investments.

According to Engku Rabiah Adawiah, Associate Professor at Ahmad Ibrahim Kulliyyah of Laws, International Islamic University Malaysia and a member of the *Shari'ah* Advisory Council (SAC) of Central Bank of Malaysia, liabilities remain the same under Islamic law up to the amount of their capital contribution and there are no separate contracts on the basis of pure business structures, be it partnership or companies. She also states that paramount in determining liability in Islamic law is not the business structure but the actual *shirkah* contracts between the parties. She adds that if the parties want limited liability, they may choose *shirkah al-inan* or *mudhārabah* and if they want unlimited liability, they may choose *shirkah al-mufawadah*.[23]

This shows that in a *mushārakah* the partners may choose and negotiate on opting to limited liability or unlimited liability. Furthermore, in a *shirkah* and *mushārakah* no partner is liable for the other partners' financial liability unless permission for that responsibility is given by the other partners on behalf of the partnership. Although any partner can become an agent for all other partners for all kinds of business transactions in the partnership (not outside), no partner is financially liable for the transactions that are made personally by other partners.[24]

Two business entities are present in the private equity and venture capital industry: the limited liability company and the limited partnership. Therefore regardless of the business structure as discussed in the paragraph above, in Islamic law it is not the business structure but the actual *shirkah* contracts between the parties that determine liability. This provides a win–win situation for both parties. This is an advantage of applying *mushārakah* in venture capital and private equity funding whereby the flexibility of Islamic law gives partners the option to choose and negotiate on opting to limited liability or unlimited liability.

3.4 Application of *mushārakah* and *mudhārabah* to contemporary private equity and venture capital funding

3.4.1 Mushārakah *venture capital*

Islamic financial institutions in the private equity and venture capital industry can establish a venture capital company that is based on *mushārakah*. It is an Islamic venture capital that operates with *mushārakah* transactions. This type of venture capital can pool funds from other Muslim countries and with equity participation can share expertise and profit with the parties involved. An example is Musharaka, which was established in 2008 by Malaysia Venture Capital Management (MAVCAP), the venture capital arm of the Ministry of Finance Malaysia. Musharaka has RM35 million, with 30 million from MAVCAP and 5 million from other investors. This is an excellent opportunity to expand

Islamic venture capital across Muslim countries and attract entrepreneurs with brilliant ideas.

3.4.2 *Diminishing* mushārakah *as an exit strategy*
It is appropriate and viable for the diminishing *mushārakah* to be applied as an exit mechanism for companies at the start-up stage because in the later stages invested companies have a higher value and prefer to exit using other exit mechanisms that will provide them with a higher return. Using diminishing *mushārakah* as an exit strategy, the price per unit of the share cannot be fixed according to the promise of the entrepreneur to purchase from the venture capital company because whether the business is a success or not, the entrepreneur has to pay that amount. The price is evaluated based on actual profit and the invested company's value and performance.

Diminishing *mushārakah* as an exit strategy is applicable as long as the venture capital company can obtain the target return and the invested company has a large amount of cash. Otherwise it can provide a win–win situation for the parties involved depending on the venture capital company's objective and the value extracted by them. Through diminishing *mushārakah* the payments are more affordable for the entrepreneur since this method of exiting is suited to short-term rather than long-term investments. Diminishing *mushārakah* as an exit strategy is further discussed in Chapter 6.

3.4.3 *Angel investors*
A group of investors or business angels who are experienced and have a lot of money provide capital and knowledge in business and can assist the entrepreneurs with their business management. A pool of angel investors is established, making it easier for the entrepreneurs to network with them.

These angel investors can assist in establishing businesses at the seed and start-up stages. This is structured by applying funds that are based on *mushārakah* and *mudhārabah* modes of financing. The angel investor can choose to engage in the management of the business with the entrepreneur or become a sleeping partner and only provide capital to the entrepreneur. Other than that, these pools of investors may be interested in *Shari'ah* compliant investments and financing structures and this can further develop small and medium-sized enterprises in most Muslim countries. These angel investors may be from another country, which is advantageous as it helps bridge the financial gap between Muslim countries. Other than encouraging international trade between Muslim countries it is also good for establishing business relations through partnerships from small-business financing.

3.4.4 *Islamic debt in leveraged buyouts*

Islamic banking and finance has made good progress in the banking sector and is slowly making its way in the private equity sector. This demonstrates innovations in terms of structuring Islamic financial instruments in areas of finance other than the banking sector. For example, the development and growth of *Shari'ah* compliant private equity funding in the Middle East and Asia is rising.

An example of *Shari'ah* compliant private equity in practice is the Aston Martin investment undertaken by Investment Dar in partnership with the Kuwait investment and wealth management group ADEEM. The deal was structured to enable Investment Dar to acquire a controlling 50.2 per cent stake for US\$464.16 million, while ADEEM, which is also *Shari'ah* compliant, acquired a smaller stake, and the Ford Motor Company, the seller, retained a US\$77 million operating stake. Ford has suffered substantial losses in its United States operations and the sale of Aston Martin was the first of its global disposals to reduce its accumulating debt. A conventional private equity structure was employed but Aston Martin was a permissible investment under *Shariʿah* and there was no leveraging of the deal by Investment Dar or ADEEM. The *Shariʿah* compliant structure that was applied in this case was a *murabaha* commodity structure, based on a profit- and loss-sharing mode of financing.

However, the application of Islamic bonds or *sukuk* in the private equity sector, especially at the consolidation stage where companies are acquired through LBOs, remains non-existent. This provides an opportunity for investors to structure their funds using a *Shariʿah* compliant method, especially at the consolidation stage where the focus is on leveraged buyout funds which involves high yield bonds plus buy and build strategies. Many factors need to be taken into consideration when applying Islamic bonds for LBOs. For example, the value of the company, current market conditions, industry growth, exit mechanism performance, marketability, infrastructure and legal issues. The types of *sukuk* that can be a potential financial instrument for an Islamic LBO are *murabaha*, *ijarah*, *mushārakah* and *salam istisna*. Using Islamic debt in the leveraged buyout process is further discussed in Chapter 6.

3.5 Conclusion

Shariʿah compliant private equity has paved the way with promising profitability; however Islamic venture capital that focuses on start-ups still remains inactive. To date there is only one Islamic venture capital fund, established in Malaysia. *Shariʿah* based as opposed to *Shariʿah* compliant contracts or funding have been discussed in order to focus on innovation in structuring financial structures in the Islamic venture capital and private equity funding, innovation that is promising in terms of funds.

Notes

1. Muhammad Taqi Usmani, *An Introduction to Islamic Finance* (Alphen aan den Rijn: Kluwer Law International, 2002), p. 20.
2. Ibid. p. 21.
3. Abdul Azim Islahi, *Economic Concepts of Ibn Taimiyah* (Leicester: The Islamic Foundation, 1998), p. 156.
4. Engku Rabiah Adawiah, 'Development of partnership structure and limited liability regime: an Islamic law perspective', presented at the International Conference on Law and Commerce, Kuala Lumpur, June 2002.
5. Muhammad Nejatullah Siddiqi, *Partnership and Profit-sharing in Islamic Law* (Leicester: The Islamic Foundation, 1985), p. 49.
6. Adiwarman A. Karim, 'Incentive-compatible constraints for Islamic banking: some lessons from Bank Muamalat', in Munawar Iqbal and David T. Llewellyn (eds), *Islamic Banking and Finance* (Cheltenham: Edward Elgar Publishing, 2002), p. 102.
7. Ibid.
8. Rodney Wilson, 'Innovation in the structuring of Islamic sukuk securities', Islamic Economics and Finance Module, Durham University, spring 2005.
9. Rodney Wilson, 'Mushārakah and mudharabah', presented at FTC Training for the Association of Merchant Banks in Malaysia, 2 June 2005.
10. Sami Al-Suwailem, *A Potential Model of Mushārakah* (Jeddah: King Abdulaziz University Academic Publication Center, Graduate Studies and Academic Research Vice-Deanship, n.d.), http://www.kaau.edu.sa/CENTERS/SPC/page-091.htm (retrieved 21 December 2009).

11. Saad Al-Harran, 'Leading issues in Islamic banking and finance', in Saad Al-Harran (ed.), *Mushārakah Financing: Concept and Application* (Subang Jaya: Pelanduk Publications, 1995), pp. 2–24.

12. Chris Bovaird, *Introduction to Venture Capital Finance* (London: Pitman Publishing, 1990), p. 7.

13. Muhammad Nejatullah Siddiqi, *Partnership and Profit-Sharing in Islamic Law* (Leicester: The Islamic Foundation, 1985), p. 22.

14. Ibid. p. 19.

15. Saad, 'Leading issues in Islamic banking and finance', p. 8.

16. Usmani, *An Introduction to Islamic Finance*, p. 38.

17. Ibid. p. 39.

18. Ibid. p. 40.

19. Ibid. p. 11.

20. Muhammad Taqi Usmani, 'Mushārakah', 2000, http://www.failaka.com/Library/Articles/Usmani%20-%20Musharaka.pdf (retrieved 21 November 2010).

21. Ibid.

22. Saad, 'Leading issues in Islamic banking and finance', p. 8.

23. Adawiah, 'Development of partnership structure and limited liability regime'.

24. Siddiqi, *Partnership and Profit-Sharing in Islamic Law*, p. 49.

CHAPTER 4

POTENTIAL AND LIMITATIONS OF *SHARI'AH* COMPLIANT PRIVATE EQUITY AND ISLAMIC VENTURE CAPITAL

This chapter explores those criteria that must be met when establishing a *Shari'ah* compliant private equity funding and Islamic venture capital industry, including company structure and investment criteria. It looks at establishing a robust industry, focusing on economic conditions, the legal system and financial infrastructure. The limitations of the *Shari'ah* compliant industry are compared to those of the conventional private equity and venture capital industry, so as to highlight the competitive advantage of the former.

4.1 Company structure

This section provides examples of the types of firm operating in the private equity and venture capital industry: limited partnerships, corporate venture capital firms, and angel investors.

4.1.1 *Limited partnerships*

In a limited partnership, the general partners (GPs) manage the company and the investors are the limited partners. Limited partners do not take part actively in the management: they invest their money for a specific time period and obtain returns when this period is over. They have no control over funds. In this case, the active partner is the general partner, who manages the funds and investments. The limited partner is the passive partner.

The advantages of a limited partnership include:

- Limited partners provide a legal structure to the formation of the business. From a capital investment perspective, the limited partners' liability is dependent upon the amount of capital invested. There are no limitations as to the amount of dividends that the general partners may receive from the business. General partners of a limited partnership may be in the form of another person or company.
- As a separate legal entity, limited partners may own property, sue and be sued in the limited partner's name.

The disadvantages of a limited partnership include:

- In a limited partnership there must be at least one general partner and it is the general partner that incurs unlimited liability.
- As in any partnership, a limited partnership must draft a partnership agreement, which administers how the business is run. In a limited partnership the partnership agreement must state a date of termination.
- Since a limited partnership is a legal entity, the formation of a limited partnership requires more legal documentation than in a general partnership.

4.1.2 Corporate venture capital firms

Corporate venture capital firms act more like a company than do limited partnerships but are still similar to a partnership. Some large banks have this type of venture capital firm. The management of the corporate venture capital firm reports to the CEO. These firms are subsidiaries of the organisation and provide capital for start-ups and other potential businesses.

The advantages of corporate venture capital include:

- Limited liability for the people who run the corporation. Shareholders of the corporation are not liable for the debts and obligations of the company.
- The corporation has an unlimited life. The corporation will continue to exist even if the shareholders die, exit the business or if there is change in ownership.
- It is easy to raise capital through the issuance of shares.
- Tax advantages.
- Losses from the corporation cannot be deducted from the owner's personal income.

The disadvantages of corporate venture capital include:

- Two tax returns, one for the business and one for personal income.
- Complicated registration procedures and high set-up fees.
- An arduous process in maintaining transparency and corporate governance due to size.

4.1.3 Angel investors

Angel investors are wealthy individuals who provide funds to start-up companies. They take part actively in the management of the business and through their experience add value to the investee or invested companies. An angel investor also puts funds into other venture capital to invest in potential businesses.

In the venture capital and private equity industry most companies are limited liability companies and limited partnerships. For example, the venture capitalists listed and registered in the Securities Commission are all companies with limited liability, with abbreviations such as Sdn Bhd (Sendirian Berhad) (private limited companies) and Bhd (Berhad) (semi-government companies). Though most venture capitalists in Malaysia are companies with limited liability, the Employment Providence Fund Malaysia's private equity section is structured on a limited partnership basis.

Most private equity funds in the Middle East are *Shari'ah* compliant structures based on *mushārakah* and *mudharabah*.[1] The offshore funds meanwhile are structured as limited partnerships.[2] In the limited partnership structure, the general partner manages the funds. This structure is still within *Shari'ah* guidelines and similar to the *mudharabah* structure.[3] Some scholars do not accept conventional business structures such as the limited partnership or corporate venture capital; instead they only accept *mushārakah* and *mudharabah* business structures.[4]

A review of the business structures in private equity and venture capital companies leads us to one factor that is important in applying the profit-and-loss-sharing instruments, that is, the type of agreement or business contract regardless of the business structure. Islamic law allows the flexibility of structuring a contract to be applied in a venture capital or private equity fund.

According to Engku Rabiah Adawiah, liabilities remain the same under Islamic law up to the amount of their capital contribution and there are no separate contracts on the basis of pure business structure, be it partnership or companies. She states that paramount in determining liability in Islamic law is not the business structure, but the actual *shirkah* contracts between the parties. She adds that if the parties want limited liability, they may choose *shirkah al-inan* or *mudhārabah*, while if they want unlimited liability, they may choose *shirkah al-mufawadah*. This demonstrates that the partners may choose and negotiate on opting to limited liability or unlimited liability in Islamic law. Furthermore, in a *shirkah* and *mushārakah* no partner is liable for the other partners' financial liability unless the other partners agree to this on behalf of the partnership. Although any partner can become an agent for all other partners for all kinds of business transactions in the partnership (not outside), no partner is financially liable for the transactions that are made personally by other partners.[5]

Therefore, what determines liability in Islamic law is not to do with the business structure, but the actual *shirkah* contracts between the parties. The result is a win–win situation for both parties through the flexibility of determining their contracts and business structure. This is an advantage of applying profit-and-loss-sharing instruments in the venture capital and private equity company. The flexibility of Islamic law gives partners the options to choose and negotiate on structuring their agreement and achieving one that will benefit both parties.

4.2 Investment criteria

This section looks at the criteria considered by venture capital companies before making any decision to invest in a company. For example, Kaplan and Strömberg's research shows that venture capitalists consider the attractiveness and risks of the business, management and deal terms as well as expected post-investment monitoring.[6] A research review by Khanin, Baum, Mahto, Raj and Heller identified the most important decision criteria of investment in new ventures as discussed in previous literature, such as a top management team, market, product, risk, deal and competition.[7] For *Shari'ah* compliant private equity and Islamic venture capital to operate well, it is vital that these criteria are met and used as a benchmark.

General criteria include:

- management
- financial information and valuation
- market potential
- growth
- industry

4.2.1 *Management*

Management criteria focus on the human resources managing the business, such as the entrepreneurs – in this case on whether the entrepreneurs have the necessary skills, qualifications and attitude. The entrepreneurs' working experience is also taken into account. Ensuring that the entrepreneur has the necessary skills for managing a business, possesses the right qualifications and is motivated and trustworthy allows the following question to be answered: is the management committed to enhancing the value of the company? This also provides an insight into the additional criteria that may be needed by *Shari'ah* compliant private equity and Islamic venture capital companies. Venture capital companies back only good management teams and the most important reason for a venture capital company investing in a business is belief in its management team.[8] It is important that the management is experienced, qualified and has the skills and the drive to bring the company to another level. Based on the Middle East and North Africa (MENA) Private Equity Confidence Survey, the quality of the team and the management's track record and reputation are key factors for the growth of the private equity industry in the MENA region. Private equity firms can steer portfolio companies towards new markets and increase market share in these new markets.[9]

4.2.2 *Financial information and valuation*

Financial evaluation of invested companies takes into consideration the previous performance of a company in assessing its financial robustness and solvency. One may want to assess the company's financial record, forecast and analysis. However, this may apply to companies seeking funds at the later stages whereby the company is more established and already has products and services. Calculating and forecasting on value creation makes more sense because it does not bear a high risk of losing the business compared to businesses in the early stages. Financial valuation is also an important factor in terms of the venture capital companies' valuation of the invested companies and whether they are able to obtain a return from the investment. It is also important in determining the value of the invested company and the venture capital companies' portfolios.

4.2.3 *Market potential, growth and industry*

A consideration of market potential and the industry in which the business operates is important in assessing where the company stands in the market. In Malaysia, information technology and manufacturing are sectors highly invested in by the government and also by private venture capital companies. Since the establishment of the multimedia super corridor, the ICT industry has boomed in Malaysia. Based on the MENA Private Equity Confidence Survey, the pharmaceutical, biotechnology and healthcare sectors make up 26 per cent of private equity investments. Consumer and retail sectors make up 14 per cent.[10]

Growth in the investment is an important consideration when selecting an investment. There are many venture capital companies in Malaysia mandated by the government that focus on the early stage. For example, Malaysian Venture Capital Management Bhd. (MAVCAP) is mandated by the finance ministry and the Malaysian Development Corporation (MDC) for ICT ventures as well as the Malaysian Technology Development Corporation (MTDC) for non-ICT ventures. Support is given by the government to help reduce the risk of the company failing, hence to increase growth. Opportunities in the Middle East are even greater: due to the oil price increase and the Gulf Cooperative Council (GCC), nations experienced gross domestic product (GDP) growth of 6.1 per cent between 2004 and 2007.[11] KPMG estimated liquidity in the GCC to be around US$2.3 trillion.[12]

Therefore it is evident that management, financial information and valuation, market potential, growth and industry are the main considerations when selecting an investment. These criteria give an idea of what is needed of an investment and the same criteria should be applied to *Shari'ah* compliant funds, and in particular *Shari'ah* compliant private equity and Islamic venture capital financing. Selection criteria are vital for investment success and solid business relationships between the venture capital companies and the invested companies.

4.2.4 *Differences between* Shari'ah *compliant private equity funds and conventional funds*

Some differences between *Shari'ah* compliant private equity funding/Islamic venture capital funding and conventional private equity funding relate to the investment and the target company's financial ratio. Those industries or sectors of investment not permitted for *Shari'ah* compliant funds are listed in the *Guidelines and Best Practices on Islamic Venture Capital* [*sic*] from the Securities Commission Malaysia:

- financial services based on *riba* (interest)
- gambling and gaming
- the manufacture or sale of non-*halal* products or related products
- conventional insurance
- entertainment activities that are not permitted according to *Shari'ah* law
- the manufacture or sale of tobacco-based products or related products
- stockbroking or share trading in non-*Shari'ah* compliant securities
- hotels and resorts
- by *ijtihad*, other activities the *Shari'ah* adviser may deem non-permissible

In terms of financial ratio, target companies may invest in several interest-bearing financial instruments. Therefore a benchmark must exist in order to ensure *Shari'ah* compliancy before an investment is made. The following methodology was established by Mufti Taqi Usmani, Professor Saleh Tug and Sheikh Mohammad Al-Tayyed Al Najar to develop the Dow Jones Islamic Index in 1999:[13]

- **Total debt**. Excludes investments when total interest-based debt divided by 12-month average market capitalisation exceeds (or is equal to) 33 per cent.
- **Total interest-nearing securities and cash**. Excludes investments when total cash and interest-bearing

securities divided by 12-month average market capitalisation exceeds (or is equal to) 33 per cent.

- **Accounts receivable.** Excludes investments in target companies if accounts receivable divided by total assets is greater than (or is equal to) 33 per cent.

If a *Shari'ah* compliant private equity company invests in a target company with accounts receivable of more than 33 per cent, the investment is not *Shari'ah* compliant. The same applies with total debt and total interest-nearing securities and cash.

Aside from adhering to *Shari'ah* compliancy standards on the industry and financial ratios, a *Shari'ah* advisor has to be appointed for *Shari'ah* compliant investments in private equity and venture capital. Based on the *Guidelines and Best Practices on Islamic Venture Capital* from the Securities Commission Malaysia, the *Shari'ah* advisor bears these responsibilities:

- to ensure that all aspects of the Islamic venture capital such as portfolio management, trade practices and operational matters comply with *Shari'ah* law
- to provide *Shari'ah* expertise and guidance on matters relating to documentation, structuring and investment principles
- to review and scrutinise compliance reports prepared by *Shari'ah* compliance officers or any investment transaction report
- to provide written opinion and periodic reports

The differences are not that many and some concepts and operations of private equity and venture capital financing remain the same. The main difference is that one is *Shari'ah* compliant and the other is not, which mainly concerns the financial instruments used for reinvestments or for funding the business. Nevertheless, this adds to the list of financing options available in the private equity and venture capital industry. The choice remains with the client as to which financing options best suit their investment appetite.

4.3 Key conditions for *Shari'ah* compliant private equity funding and Islamic venture capital

This section looks at the economic conditions, legal systems, financial infrastructures and human resources that are crucial in establishing and developing the Islamic venture capital and *Shari'ah* compliant private equity industry in specific regions.

4.3.1 *Economic conditions in the MENA region, South East Asia and the UK*

Private equity in the Middle East is still in its infancy; however the industry is growing at a promising rate each year. According to the Gulf Venture Capital Association (GVCA) Annual Report 2008, a fund of US$6.4 billion was raised, boosting the private equity industry in the Middle East.[14] Investors in the Middle East are from wealthy families who are high net worth individuals. They own single- and multi-family businesses, local investment banks and sovereign wealth funds.[15] Sovereign wealth funds make up most of the investment in the private equity industry in the Middle East, whereby the key players are investors from Western countries.[16] However, companies such as Investment Dar, Investcorp and Gulf Finance are also competitive when compared to the conventional private equity companies, for example in Investment Dar's buyout of Aston Martin.

The Islamic private equity industry is worth US$3 billion through investments mainly in the MENA region.[17] This is a small amount compared to the Islamic banking and finance industry, which is worth US$800 billion.[18] Nevertheless, this shows that there are opportunities to further develop *Shari'ah* compliant private equity and Islamic venture capital in the Middle East. According to the World Islamic Banking Competitiveness Report 2008, US$3.4 trillion was available in the region for investment locally and overseas.[19] At the same time, Middle East investors demand that overseas investments establish links to the Middle East and the North Africa region whereby target companies agree to the production and distribution of their product in the MENA region.[20] Oil prices are increasing and the Gulf regions are benefiting from the revenue. There is no doubt that there is a high amount of liquidity in the Middle East region. This will provide a good platform for establishing *Shari'ah* compliant private equity and venture capital funds to develop small businesses and expand industries.

In Malaysia, the venture capital industry began with the establishment of the Malaysian Ventures Berhad in 1984. The number of venture capital companies rose to six in 1990 and to thirteen by 1992. The numbers then soared after the establishment of the multimedia super corridor where incubators were set up to nurture small companies in the technology industry. Tax incentives for the venture capital industry also contributed to the steady growth of the industry. By the end of 1998, the number of venture capital companies registered with Bank Negara Malaysia had almost doubled, increasing to twenty-three. Venture capital financing is increasingly recognised as an alternative source of funds in Malaysia, simply because the cost of borrowing is high and the economy unpredictable.

The venture capital industry has brought tremendous growth and investment opportunities to the Malaysian economy. According to Zarinah Anwar, writing in 2006:

At the end of 2005, the number of committed funds has risen to RM2.6 billion from RM2.1 billion in 2003. The number of investee companies has also grown by 30% since 2003. Statistics also show that the private sector is fast taking over the role of Government as the prime source for these funds. It has become more apparent that Malaysia is now experiencing a strong acceptance of venture capital, as an alternative vehicle into the mainstream capital market products of debt, equity and derivative instruments.[21]

These figures clearly show the importance of venture capital financing in Malaysia. This also provides opportunities for foreign capital to flow into Malaysia's economy. The following are recommendations for the venture capital industry in Malaysia according to the Financial Sector Master Plan:

- To chart the strategic direction for the Malaysian venture capital industry and act as a single reference point for all government initiatives and incentives.
- To coordinate and ensure other elements develop in tandem with the venture capital industry.
- To increase the availability of venture capital financing as well as stimulate more new ventures, especially in the ICT industry.
- To ensure effective use of funds; consideration is given to the management of funds being outsourced to private sectors/corporations with necessary expertise.
- To ensure that tax incentives in the form of tax deductions are equivalent to the amount of investments made in approved venture capital companies at start-up, seed capital and early-stage financing.
- To encourage more companies to list on MESDAQ (Malaysian Exchange of Securities Dealing and Automated Quotation) and build interest and market

liquidity and make exit mechanisms for venture capital companies more attractive to increase venture capital investment.

• To encourage Malaysian venture capital companies to form smart partnerships with venture capital companies in the Organisation of Islamic Cooperation (OIC) to help enhance the pool of available venture capital funds in Malaysia.[22]

MESDAQ was launched in 1997 to provide a platform for companies in the ICT industry to raise equity capital and to promote the venture capital industry by providing an exit mechanism for their investments. On top of the rec-ommendations listed in the Financial Market Master Plan, the Malaysian Venture Capital Association (MVCA) was also established in 1995 with the objective of promoting and developing the Malaysian venture capital industry. One of the MVCA's initiatives was the founding of the Venture Capital Consultative Council (VCCC), in collaboration with the National Economic Action Council of the prime minister's department.

Under the Ninth Malaysian Plan, Malaysia allocated RM1.6 billion (US$500 million) for the venture capital and private equity sector. In 2007 there were 52 registered ven-ture capital companies in Malaysia, rising to 56 in 2008. In 2007 there were 46 registered venture capital management companies (VCMCs), rising to 52 in 2008. The VCMCs are responsible for managing the funds.

Most of the deals were within the expansion/growth stage, totalling RM298,632 million (62 per cent of the overall investment for 2008). Second largest was the early stage, at RM82,785 million (17 per cent of the overall investment for 2008). The total amount invested in com-panies at the seed stage represented only 3 per cent of total investments made in 2008. (Please refer to Table 2.4 on p. 22.)

Brunei, through its Ministry of Finance, formed an alliance with SBI Holdings Inc., a Japanese financial services provider, to establish a fund management company expected to handle private equity funds, including *Sharia'ah* compliant vehicles.[23] According to the *Brunei Times*, Brunei, as the centre of and gateway to the Islamic world in Southeast Asia, is surrounded by various opportunities to grow further and diversify its economy.[24] This clearly shows that economically Brunei has an attractive market for private equity where it can generate growth for the services provided by SBI Holdings Inc.

Following this, Belgium has considered Brunei as a platform for investments into the Islamic finance sector through Islamic venture capital funds.[25] 'According to Marc Deschamps, member of Wallonia's Foreign Trade and Investment Agency (AWEX), Brunei is the country's most suitable potential partner in the South East Asia [*sic*].'[26] Deschamps also mentioned that venture capital, which is part of the conventional finance closest to Islamic law, is a viable product to launch in Belgium given its legislation and tax rules, which makes it very attractive.[27] '[T]he Brunei Economic Development Board (BEDB) was formed on November 26, 2001 with the objective to stimulate the growth, expansion and development of the economy by promoting Brunei Darussalam as an investment destination.'[28]

The BEDB listed points answering the question 'Why Brunei?', aimed at attracting potential investors to Brunei. The list covers areas of the economy and political stability such as a robust infrastructure, tax incentives, an excellent standard of living, low crime rates and pollution, flexible regulations for starting up businesses and for investment inflow, and a business-friendly environment where systems are efficient and fast.[29]

The United Kingdom has one of the best-established financial systems in the world. The United Kingdom government has opened its financial system to provide Islamic banking and services to the world, which shows robust financial regulation. Government initiatives have enabled the fiscal and regulatory framework in the United Kingdom for Islamic banking and finance. The initiatives include:

- The removal in 2003 of double tax on Islamic mortgages and the extension of tax relief on Islamic mortgages to companies, as well as individuals.
- Reform of arrangements for issues of bonds so that returns and income payments can be treated 'as if' interest. This makes London a more attractive location for issuing and trading Sukuk.
- Initiatives by the Financial Service Authority to ensure that regulatory treatment of Islamic finance is consistent with its statutory objectives and principles.[30]

In the United Kingdom there are five *Shari'ah* compliant banks, making the UK Europe's leading provider of Islamic banking and finance.[31] There are also local banks with Islamic windows. For instance, HSBC bank through its Islamic finance HSBC Amanah provides home financing based on Islamic guidelines. The European Islamic Investment Bank provides investment banking services which consist of private equity, trade finance and asset management. This shows that the United Kingdom provides services in the area of *Shari'ah* compliant private equity. Gatehouse Bank also has investment banking services and took part in the underwriting process for the buyout of Aston Martin. To date the United Kingdom has established a strong market for the Islamic banking and finance industry due to its government's supportive policies that help to nurture the Islamic banking and finance industry and to operate in congruence with the conventional industries.

The United Kingdom has proven that its financial industry is quick to pioneer and develop new products and services such as Islamic banking and finance. This would not have been possible without a strong economy and a dynamic financial market. The flexibility of being able to alter and adjust its current banking regulations in accordance with Islamic principles makes the United Kingdom attractive for investors around Europe and the Middle East. According to the Financial Services Authority (November 2007), 'The UK financial services industry has a proven record of developing and delivering new products and a large pool of legal, accounting and financial engineering skills on which to draw.'[32]

4.3.2 *Legal systems*

The legal system of a specific country has to accommodate *Shari'ah* law in terms of *fiqh muamalat*. The contract used in the investment deal has to abide by *Shari'ah* law. This is to ensure that the procedures and investment environment are *Shari'ah* compliant. The best example of this is the United Kingdom government's policy for the development of the Islamic banking and finance sector in the United Kingdom. In 2010 there were 20 law firms in the UK providing services relating to Islamic finance.[33] According to a Financial Services Authority 2007 report on Islamic Finance in the UK, 'English law is already the preferred legal jurisdiction for many Islamic finance transactions.'[34] This is a big advantage to the United Kingdom in terms of expanding and marketing Islamic financial services. From these examples it can be seen how dynamic the legal system is in the United Kingdom in terms of widening opportunities for establishing markets in the Islamic banking and finance sector.

In the case of Malaysia, where Islamic jurisprudence is concerned, separate Islamic legislation and banking regulations operate side by side with those for the conventional banking system. 'Islamic banks in Malaysia are regulated by the Islamic Banking Act 1983. The Islamic Banking Act 1983 is governed by the Central Bank of Malaysia.'[35]

Any cases involving Islamic banking and finance products are covered under *Shari'ah* law or the civil law. The Malaysian government structured a *Shari'ah* Framework whereby Islamic financial institutions operate in an environment that is effective and conducive. The most important point in this matter is to ensure that there is an avenue for seeking advice and solutions dealing with transactions concerning Islamic banking and finance products.

Two new instruments were introduced in 2011 to enhance the variety of instruments for liquidity management in the Islamic money market in Malaysia.[36] The first was the Bank Negara Monetary Notes-Istithmar (BNMN-Istithmar) and the second the Bank Negara Monetary Notes-Bai Bithaman Ajil (BNMN-BBA).[37]

In the same year, the Sasana Kijang was established. It is a modern centre of excellence for central banking and financial services which promotes regional and international collaboration.[38]

Malaysia also remained the global leader in sukuk issuances, capturing 66 percent or $94 billion of total global sukuk outstanding as at end of 2010. Bursa Malaysia is currently the largest sukuk listing exchange in the world with a value of $27.7

billion as at end of 2010, exceeding that of any other leading international financial center. [39]

4.3.3 Financial infrastructure

Financial infrastructure is vital when it comes to developing a *Shari'ah* compliant private equity and Islamic venture capital industry, in particular *Shari'ah* compliance procedures, profitability and potential return, risk management, and marketability. The *Shari'ah* compliance procedures highlight the compliancy of the fund and the processes involved in structuring the investment deal. This involves appointing *Shari'ah* advisors, concentrating on *Shari'ah* compliant business, operations, activities and instruments, and ensuring that the return is in capital gain and not interest. The investment and financial instruments used must be free from *riba* and the venture must be based on profit-sharing.

For *Shari'ah* compliant private equity and Islamic venture capital financing, the screening process requires a *Shari'ah* scholar, who may sit on the board of directors or be appointed as one of the managers to ensure that the operations and activities of the venture capital company comply with *Shari'ah* principles. *Shari'ah* scholars are appointed by the *Shari'ah* scholar advisory council of the respective country. Therefore *Shari'ah* advisors/scholars play a vital role in:

- analysing the investment to ensure it is *halal*
- analysing the contracts and agreements (avoiding *gharar*)
- analysing the pricing of the investment and how it is structured and ensuring that it is interest-free
- performing a *Shari'ah* compliance review for pre-IPO (initial public offering – the first sale of stock by a company to the public; see section 6.2.1) securities

- analysing that the instruments used are *Shari'ah* compliant

In terms of the contract and agreement, this does not need to be completely free of *gharar*. For example, this is stated in the resolutions of the Securities Commission Malaysia *Shari'ah* Advisory Council (SAC), whereby *gharar* and *ghubn* are two negative elements that can unfavourably affect a contract. However, if this occurs in a small amount, Islamic jurisprudence considers this to be normal and so it does not affect the contract's goodwill. In Malaysia, to further promote the Islamic capital market, *Shari'ah* compliance reviews for pre-IPO have been implemented. Previously the compliance reviews were subject to listed companies on the Bursa Malaysia. The contract written should be as precise as possible, transparent and understood by the invested company. In relation to contract and agreement, a lawyer well versed in *Shari'ah* law should help ensure that the agreements are based on Islamic law.

The instruments used must be *Shari'ah* compliant. Ordinary shares must be *Shari'ah* compliant and not loan stock or cumulative preference shares (CPS). Return from the investment should also be *Shari'ah* compliant whereby returns must not be interest-based. However, this depends on the stage of the investments. In the early stage some investments use preference shares which result in interest; therefore they are not *Shari'ah* compliant. As for the later stages, ordinary shares may be used for the investment and then the returns are through capital gains. This is *Shari'ah* compliant. Therefore, Islamic venture capital and *Shari'ah* compliant private equity companies are not limited to using ordinary shares only. Examples of instruments that are *Shari'ah* permissible include commodity *murabaha*, convertible preference shares, redeemable preference shares, and ordinary shares. However, again this depends on the stage of the investment and the industry.

In terms of profit and return on the investment, *Shari'ah* compliant private equity and Islamic venture capital companies have to compete with the conventional product and market. They should be attractive when compared to other funds on the market. This raises questions concerning the potential rate of return and dividend payment that is obtained through *Shari'ah* compliant funds and whether this creates value.

Regarding risk mitigation, the investment process must be transparent for both investor and investee. They should be aware of the risks involved and both must find ways to mitigate them.

Demand by clients also plays a major role in ensuring the success of an Islamic financial fund. There must be a market for *Shari'ah* compliant funds in private equity or venture capital. Information on the products and services in relation to *Shari'ah* compliant private equity and Islamic venture capital should be available and accessible. This assists the management and the invested company in terms of knowledge of the *Shari'ah* compliant instrument used.

In relation to the points above, a country's government must provide the infrastructure and financial support for developing an Islamic banking and finance industry as this will assist in structuring *Shari'ah* compliant private equity funds and Islamic venture capital companies.

While Malaysia holds the largest market for Islamic private debt securities, in the case of equity financing, the number is still small. Other than having the largest market, Malaysia develops its Islamic banking and finance industry. Malaysia therefore has the infrastructure for *Shari'ah* compliant private equity and Islamic venture capital companies in terms of financial infrastructure, regulatory framework and resources. A tax review for special purpose vehicles for Islamic financing has been a good platform for starting such funds. In Malaysia, the *Shari'ah* Advisory Council of the Securities Commission in Malaysia is responsible for ensuring the *Shari'ah* compliancy of the investment, instruments used and contracts and agreement, while on the legal side, a lawyer well versed in *Shari'ah* law may be of assistance in ensuring that the agreements are based on Islamic law.

In the Middle East, for instance, the GVCA was established in the Kingdom of Bahrain in June 2005 to foster growth in the area of private equity and venture capital. The association will strive to:

- promote and advocate VC/PE as a vital industry, contributing to economic growth
- facilitate communication and networking among stakeholders
- gather and disseminate industry statistics and information
- develop and promote professional and ethical codes of conduct
- foster professional development and [a] learning environment[40]

A suitable financial infrastructure will make a country's *Shari'ah* compliant private equity and Islamic venture capital industry more competitive for foreign direct investment (FDI), thus contributing to economic growth. It may also assist in developing more financial structures for *Shari'ah* compliant funds.

4.3.4 *Human resources*
There is a need for Islamic universities and colleges to produce more Islamic scholars and graduates to become

educators, managers and entrepreneurs; to administer knowledge pertaining to managing banks; to act as financial intermediaries; and to start up businesses in the *Shari'ah* compliant private equity and Islamic venture capital industry. There is also the need to establish more Islamic banks and other financial institutions to cater for that. This also means that more human resource is required. Malaysia and the United Kingdom are the leading providers of Islamic banking and finance courses at academic and professional levels. Academic and professional institutions include:

- International Islamic University Malaysia
- University Sains Islam Malaysia
- University Malaya
- Universiti Utara Malaysia
- Universiti Kebangsaan Malaysia
- Islamic Banking and Finance Institute Malaysia
- Centre for Research and Training
- Al Madinah International University
- International Centre for Education in Islamic Finance (INCEIF)[41]

Some of the Islamic banking and finance professional courses offered in the United Kingdom are through the Chartered Institute of Management Accountants, Chartered Institute for Securities and Investment, and the Institute of Islamic Banking and Insurance. In addition there are many academic institutions in the United Kingdom offering courses in Islamic banking and finance, for example Durham University. In 2009 there were 55 institutions offering Islamic banking and finance education and training in the United Kingdom, while there were 24 in Malaysia.[42] Such developments assist in providing skills for the Islamic banking and finance industry worldwide.

4.4 Limitations of *Shari'ah* compliant funding

The limitations of *Shari'ah* instruments provide an insight into issues relating to *Shari'ah* compliant funding in the venture capital and private equity setting. The areas of limitation touch on the process of structuring the *Shari'ah* compliant instrument, the reinvestment of capital gains, returns, and the size of fund.

Based on the MENA Private Equity Confidence Survey (October 2009), governance is identified as a challenge and barrier to overcome in developing the private equity industry in the MENA (15 per cent of the overall survey). Market regulation comprises 14 per cent, followed by human capital deficiencies. Legal framework variances accounts for 11 per cent of the overall survey.[43]

Governance, as seen in the survey, is important in structuring *Shari'ah* compliant funding in the venture capital and private equity setting as the contract has to be transparent in terms of pricing and the rights and responsibilities of the parties involved. The documentation and contracts should be well understood by the parties involved before any agreement takes place, so as to avoid *gharar*.

In terms of legal framework efficiency, this will determine the pace of the investment transactions. The procedure can be slow if the parties involved do not have sound knowledge of Islamic banking and finance principles. In addition, the investors are confident if they know the funding well. This also depends on the stage of the investments. At the later stage when the target company is at the maturity level and has been in operation for several years, the investment deal is easier because the target company is about to exit.

Another limitation of *Shari'ah* compliant funding relates to reinvesting the capital gains. This may be due to a small capital market in the relevant country. This may lead to a lack of options and choice in terms of *Shariʻah* compliant securities in the Islamic capital market. The products are limited compared to the conventional capital market. In terms of return, the ability to recover the investment is important in order to remain competitive. *Shariʻah* compliant funding in a venture capital or private equity company should be able to meet the expected return of the investor.

However, this depends on many things such as industry performance, the stage of the investment and the performance of the private placement exchange in the relevant country. This also means that if the funds are small, the returns are low. However, this does not mean that *Shariʻah* compliant funding in a venture capital or private equity company is not profitable. The issue is whether it can create value to the investment. In addition, the relevant country must have a sound infrastructure in order for *Shariʻah* compliant funding in a venture capital or private equity company to be further developed. The process of structuring the investment deals must be efficient and accurate in order to remain competitive on a global scale. Nevertheless, in addition to those limitations already mentioned, it is the lack of expertise relating to private equity and Shari'ah law that most urgently needs to be addressed.

4.5 Case studies

4.5.1 India: opportunities for establishing Islamic private equity in Asia

The Bhatt Committee of 1972 opened doors to the venture capital industry in India.[44] Following this the Bhatt Committee was in charge of developing the Indian venture capital industry through an Rs1 billion venture capital fund.[45] Since then investment deals have increased through the support of the government. In the Asia region India is emerging with promising growth in the private equity industry.

Venture capital and private equity investments in India have witnessed a phenomenal growth in terms of the amount invested, from US$1.8 billion in 2004 to US$22 billion in 2007, before tapering off to US$8.1 billion in 2008. The number of deals also increased, from 80 in 2004 to 481 in 2007, slowing down to 297 in 2008.[46]

This proves that India has the infrastructure for private equity, including Islamic private equity. Middle East investors have shown interest in investing in India. One example of this is the Gulf Finance House (GFH) economic development zone, a US$10 billion development funded by GFH. According to GFH Chairman Esam Janahi, the economic development zone was an attractive investment due to India's growth in the face of the economic downturn and the state of Maharashtra and its capital city Mumbai was the ideal investment and a strategic location in India.[47]

> On completion EDZ, which comprises of three distinct components, namely Energy City, IT & Telecom City and Entertainment City, will house approximately 140,000 residents and will generate direct employment for over 250,000 people and indirect employment for as many as 750,000 people.[48]

It is evident that India has the infrastructure for establishing Islamic private equity funds for infrastructure purposes, especially in Mumbai. Furthermore, Asia has become an investment hub for the Middle East investors and infrastructure funds are one of the sources that can establish global investment opportunities.

> ## What do you think?

1. What other issues and challenges need to be addressed in order to establish Islamic private equity in India?
2. Can *Shari'ah* compliant funds be registered under current legislation?
3. What is the potential of *Shari'ah* compliant private equity and Islamic venture capital in India?

4.5.2 MENA: *Sovereign wealth funds to foster growth for* Shari'ah *compliant private equity funding*

'Sovereign wealth funds are state run investment funds that most governments use to carry out purchases of foreign assets.'[49] The high number of sovereign wealth funds (SWFs) has invited investments from abroad and the Middle East has become the avenue for private equity investing and financing worldwide. One of the largest SWFs in the MENA region is Abu Dhabi Investment Authority (ADIA) which amounts to US$875 billion. Kuwait Investment Authority has US$250 billion and Saudi Arabia has US$300 billion. Qatar Investment Authority has US$40 billion (all figures as at 2007). In the North Africa region, Libya has US$50 billion and Algeria US$42.6 billion. Many of the SWFs, especially the large ones such as ADIA, made international investments in companies like Citigroup and EFG-Hermes. The investments from the SWFs are in real estate, healthcare and education and related to infrastructure.

According to the *Private Equity and Venture Capital in the Middle East 2007 Annual Report*, most of the SWF investment goes to the financial sector.[50] 'In the last three years, the trend has been to move away from the more traditional real estate and basic material sectors to diversify the breadth of investments.'[51] However, in terms of Islamic private equity and Islamic acquisition, this would be a great opportunity to develop further such products and services in the Middle East. Also according to the report:

> Exits in the SWF market seem limited, because the market perception is that they prefer to have long-term, risk-averse portfolios and tend to pursue buy-and-hold strategies, with no short positions and perhaps no borrowing or direct lending of any kind. They probably have long horizons and, like other long-term investors, are willing to step in when asset prices fall.[52]

Therefore using SWFs for private equity investment can be a good diversification in the investment portfolio, where investments are for the long term and the process of buy and build takes place to create value to the target company. In return the investor can hold ownership in the target company. In essence this can also be carried out based on the *mushārakah* and *diminishing mushārakah* concept where management and risk are shared. The future is bright for developing more businesses and this creates employment.

What do you think?

1. What are the opportunities and challenges when it comes to establishing Islamic private equity funds through SWFs?
2. In terms of growth, can the private equity funds rival SWFs?

3. What determines the success of the private equity industry in the MENA region?

4.5.3 Luxembourg: An emerging platform for Islamic private equity in Europe

Private equity was established in Luxembourg in the 1980s with the structure of participating companies (SOPARFI: société de participation financières).[53] A survey conducted by the European Private Equity and Venture Capital Association (2006) ranked Luxembourg as the second most favourable jurisdiction in Europe for the development of the private equity industry.[54] Establishing a region to market and develop Islamic banking and finance services requires solid financial infrastructure. Luxembourg has a private equity industry with tax advantages. In 2009 Luxembourg had 53 double tax treaties.[55]

Aside from tax advantages in the Luxembourg private equity industry, there is continuous innovation in structuring funds to attract local and foreign investors, such as risk capital investment companies (SICAR: société d'investissement à capital risque) and specialised investment funds (SIFs). In 2009 there were 219 registered SICARs and 858 registered SIFs in Luxembourg.[56] The total number of SICARs incorporated in Luxembourg up to February 2011 amounts to 242. Based on the facts given, it appears that Luxembourg has an advanced private equity industry and has great potential for Islamic private equity.[57]

The procedures for structuring the funds must be *Shari'ah* compliant. Therefore a *Shari'ah* advisory board has to be present to ensure *Shari'ah* compliancy. Financial reporting with guidelines structured by the Accounting and Auditing Organisation for Islamic Financial Institutions (AAOIFI) is another crucial element when structuring a *Shari'ah* compliant fund because there are different accounting rules to certain assets in Islamic private equity. This may not be in line with the Luxembourg GAAP (Generally Accepted Accounting Principles). This detailed information has to be reported to the shareholders for due diligence.

Another challenge is to find experts in the area of Islamic private equity to structure the deals and ensure *Shari'ah* compliancy throughout the process. Nevertheless, Luxembourg remains attractive as a platform for structuring Islamic private equity funds. In 2009 there were ten *Shari'ah* compliant funds listed on the Luxembourg Stock Exchange, as well as approximately EUR12 billion of bonds listed by Gulf countries' issuers. Among them, 16 are *sukuk*s (Islamic bonds) for a total volume of approximately EUR5.2 billion.[58]

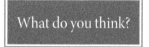

1. What other issues and challenges need to be addressed in structuring Islamic private equity in Luxembourg?
2. Can *Shari'ah* compliant funds be registered under the double tax treaties jurisdiction?
3. Which investments and industries will benefit through *Shari'ah* compliant private equity funds established in Luxembourg?

4.5.4 *United States: Islamic private equity*

To give an example of a *Shari'ah* compliant private equity fund, Guidance Financial Group, an international Islamic financial services company in the US, structured Asia's first Islamic buyout fund.[59] In September 2003, it announced the successful closing of Asia's first Islamic private equity fund. It is also *Shari'ah* advisor to the fund.[60] According to Salahuddin Ahmed: 'Guidance structured the fund through collaboration with Navis Capital Partners to offer Islamic investors in the Gulf and South East Asia the opportunity to participate in Navis's latest US$86 million round of fund raising.'[61]

What do you think?

1. What other issues and challenges need to be addressed in structuring Islamic private equity in the United States?
2. Which investments and industries will benefit through *Shari'ah* compliant private equity funds established in the United States?
3. How do the *Shari'ah* compliant private equity funds established in the United States perform?

Notes

1 Dechert on Point, *Islamic Private Equity Funds* (February 2010), p. 3, http://www.dechert.com/Islamic_Private_Equity_Funds_02-04-2010 (retrieved 6 June 2011).
2. Ibid. p. 4.
3. Ibid.
4. Paul Wouter, 'Islamic private equity fund', *Islamic Finance News*, 2008, p. 4, http://islamicfinancenews.com/pdf/private%20equity.pdf (retrieved 6 June 2011).
5. Engku Rabiah Adawiah, 'Development of partnership structure and limited liability regime: An Islamic law perspective', presented at the International Conference on Law and Commerce, Kuala Lumpur, June 2002.
6. Steven N. Kaplan and Per Strömberg, 'Characteristics,

contracts, and actions: evidence from venture capitalist analyses', *Journal of Finance*, 2004, vol. 59, no. 5, pp. 2177–210.

7. Dimitry Kahnin, J. Baum, Robert Mahto, V. Raj and Charles Heller, 'Venture capitalists' investment criteria: 40 years of research', *Small Business Institute Research Review*, 2008, vol. 35, p. 187.

8. David Gladstone and Laura Gladstone, *Venture Capital Handbook: An Entrepreneur's Guide to Raising Venture Capital* (Englewood Cliffs: Prentice Hall, 2002), p. 40.

9. Deloitte, 'Shaping up for 2010: MENA private equity confidence survey', October 2009, p. 5, http://www.deloitte. com/assets/Dcom-Lebanon/Local%20Assets/Documents/ MENA%20Private%20Equity%20Confidence%20Survey.pdf (retrieved 6 June 2011).

10. Ibid. p. 7.

11. Rafi-uddin Shikoh, 'Opportunities in Islamic private equity', 22 November 2007, p. 1, http://dinarstandard.com/ finance/opportunities-in-islamic-private-equity (retrieved 12 February 2011).

12. Ibid.

13. Wouter, 'Islamic private equity fund', p. 4.

14. GVCA, *Private Equity and Venture Capital in the Middle East 2008 Annual Report*, p. 11, http://www.kpmg.com/Global/en/ IssuesAndInsights/ArticlesPublications/Emerging-markets-MENA/Pages/Private-equity-venture-capital-Middle-East. aspx (retrieved 3 March 2011).

15. Dechert on Point, *Islamic Private Equity Funds*, p. 2.

16. Ibid. p. 6.

17. Paul McNamara, 'Islamic private equity: an untapped opportunity', Yassar Media, p. 1, http://www.ameinfo.com/205803. html (retrieved 4 March 2011).

18. Ibid. p. 2.

19. Dechert on Point, *Islamic Private Equity Funds*, p. 2.

20. Ibid.

21. Zarinah Anwar, Venture Capital Investors Forum, 21 August 2006, http://www.sc.com.my/eng/html/resources/speech/sp_20060821.html (retrieved 10 January 2010).

22. *The Financial Sector Master Plan* (n.d.), http://www.bnm.gov.my/index.php?ch=20&pg=32&ac=24 (retrieved 5 March 2010).

23. 'Japan's SBI holdings, Brunei in private equity joint venture,' *Brunei Times*, 31 March 2010, p. 1.

24. Ibid. p. 2.

25. 'Belgium eyes Brunei for Islamic venture capital', *New Horizon Global Perspective on Islamic Banking and Insurance*, 1 April 2010, p. 1, http://www.newhorizon-islamicbanking.com/index.cfm?action=view&id=10780&section=news (retrieved 4 March 2011).

26. Ibid.

27. Ibid.

28. 'Brunei Economic Development Board', http://www.brunei-directhys.net/about_brunei/brunei_economic_development.html (retrieved 12 May 2011).

29. Ibid.

30. *IFSL Research: Islamic Finance 2010*, p. 7, http://www.thecityuk.com/assets/Uploads/Islamic-finance-2010.pdf (retrieved 1 March 2011).

31. Ibid. p. 5.

32. Financial Services Authority, *Islamic Finance in the UK: Regulations and Challenges*, 2007, p. 7, http://www.fsa.gov.uk/pubs/other/islamic_finance.pdf (retrieved 5 May 2011).

33. *IFSL Research: Islamic Finance 2010*, p. 7 (retrieved 1 March 2011).

34. Financial Services Authority, *Islamic Finance in the UK*, p. 7 (retrieved 5 May 2011).

35. *Islamic Banking Act* (n.d.), http://www.mifc.com/index.php?ch=menu_law&pg=menu_law_rel&ac=55&ms=1 (retrieved 13 August 2009).

36. *Bank Negara Annual Report 2011*, p. 82, http://www.bnm.gov. my/files/publication/ar/en/2011/ar2011_book.pdf (retrieved 10 May 2012).
37. Ibid. p. 118.
38. Ibid.
39. Bank Negara Malaysia Projects Positive Outlook for Malaysia Islamic Banking System and Financial Stability in 2011, http://www.mifc.com/sift_09/newsletter/APR-2011/index.html (accessed 10 May 2010).
40. GVCA and KPMG, *Private Equity and Venture Capital in the Middle East 2007, Annual Report 2008*, p. 66, http://www.kpmg.es/docs/PrivateEqVenture.pdf (retrieved 10 May 2010).
41. Association of Islamic Banking Institutions Malaysia, http://www.aibim.com (retrieved 10 May 2010).
42. *IFSL Research: Islamic Finance 2009*, p. 1, http://www.thecity uk.com/assets/Uploads/Islamic-finance-2009.pdf (retrieved 10 May 2010).
43. Deloitte, 'Shaping up for 2010: MENA private equity confidence survey', p. 5.
44. Mansoor Durrani and Grahame Boocock, *Venture Capital, Islamic Finance and SMEs: Valuation, Structuring and Monitoring Practises in India* (New York: Palgrave Macmillan, 2006), p. 87.
45. Ibid. p. 88.
46. 'Prospects for Islamic Venture Capital Fund (IVCF) in Indian Economy', conference held 14–15 May 2011, Parliament House Annexe, New Delhi.
47. CIBAFI, '$10bn GFH economic zone launched in India', 7 March 2010, http://www.cibafi.org/NewsCenter/English/PrintPage.aspx?id=7199&Type=4 (retrieved 25 June 2011).
48. Ibid.
49. Zeinab Karake-Shalhoub, 'Private equity, Islamic finance, and sovereign wealth funds in the MENA region', *Thunderbird International Business Review*, 2008, vol. 50, no. 6, p. 365.

50. GVCA and KPMG, *Private Equity and Venture Capital in the Middle East 2007, Annual Report 2008*, p. 52.

51. Ibid. p. 30.

52. Ibid. p. 54.

53. Olivier Jordant and Farabi Zakaria, 'Islamic private equity: a new diversification for the Luxembourg private equity centre', 8 September 2009, p. 1, http://www.ey.com/LU/en/Newsroom/PR-activities/Articles/article_2009-islamic-private-equity-september09 (retrieved 10 February 2011).

54. PricewaterhouseCoopers, *Private Equity in Luxembourg*, September 2006, p. 3, http://hecpevc.files.wordpress.com/2008/07/pwc_privateequity.pdf (retrieved 10 February 2011).

55. Jordant and Zakaria, 'Islamic private equity', p. 1 (retrieved 10 February 2011).

56. Ibid.

57. Private Equity, Ernst & Young Luxembourg, 2011, p. 4, http://www.ey.com/Publication/vwLUAssets/Private_Equity_Luxembourg/$File/Private%20Equity.pdf (retrieved 4 June 2012).

58. Jordant and Zakaria, 'Islamic private equity', p. 1 (retrieved 10 February 2011).

59. Salahuddin Ahmed, *Islamic Banking and Insurance: A Global Overview* (Kuala Lumpur: AS Noordeen, 2009), pp. 384–5.

60. Ibid. p. 385.

61. Ibid.

CHAPTER 5
PROFIT-SHARING, VALUATION AND RISK MITIGATION

This chapter looks at the profit-sharing features, valuation and risk mitigation methods of *Shari'ah* compliant private equity and Islamic venture capital. These are important elements as they can create value and maximise wealth. Risk management is also discussed, to explore problems that can be overcome in order to enhance efficiency and profitability.

5.1 Profit- and loss-sharing and wealth distribution

Equity financing in the Islamic economy focuses on the profit- and loss-sharing basis. It also shares management of the business and has ownership and some control in the business through shareholding. This way it encourages partnership and joint venture to pull capital rather than borrowing. This also creates partnership between the fund suppliers and the fund demanders. However, ownership can become an issue because the pioneer of the business may have to give away huge portions of their share to the investors and may have less control in the company.

This is one important point in profit- and loss-sharing because it can be a disadvantage for the profit- and loss-sharing financial instruments such as *mushārakah* if applied in venture capital and private equity. The disadvantage in this matter would be on the entrepreneurs' side whereby they have to give up ownership and control of their company to the shareholders. However, interest is not present in this case because the equity finance investors do not have rights to interest which is to be paid at a certain date. They are to be paid in dividends and this depends on the value, growth and profitability of the business. Equity finance investors also get their returns from the capital gains of the shares sold upon exit. Two sources of equity financing are venture capital and business angels. Both are used for high-growth business, especially venture capital whereby the shares are placed in an exchange upon exit. The role of equity financing is vital in the economy as it becomes an alternative for debt financing.

Equity and efficiency are pillars in the Islamic economy. To obtain equity, instruments, *Shari'ah* guidelines, human resources and a stable political infrastructure are needed. The instruments currently widely used in Islamic banking and finance are:

- *murabaha*
- *mudhārabah*
- *mushārakah*
- *muqarada*
- *ijarah*
- *salam*
- *istisna*
- *sukuk*
- *bai bithamin ajil* (BBA)

Of the instruments listed, two are profit- and loss-sharing and equity based: *mudhārabah* and *mushārakah*. In the *mudhārabah* structure, management is not shared between the fund provider and the entrepreneur, as in the *mushārakah* structure. Management is the responsibility of the *mudharib*, the entrepreneur. In the Islamic economy the role of equity financing is important for:

- stabilising the economy through equity participation
- foreign equity capital
- promoting small and medium enterprises (SMEs), and
- lessening poverty rates and instilling brotherhood among Muslims

Stabilising the economy through equity participation such as using profit- and loss-sharing contracts such as the *mushārakah* helps to ensure fairness between the entrepreneur, investors and the partners involved. The profit- and loss-sharing and the profit rates determined by the partners are based on the amount of capital given, while the profit depends on the performance and growth of the business. The distribution of profit and return of capital between the partners, entrepreneurs and the investor is determined by what was negotiated and agreed upon.

Given the fairness of the profit- and loss-sharing feature, equity participation is a comfortable avenue for investments and joint venture between partners, investors and entrepreneurs. Equity participation in this case means cooperation between businesses within the country itself, other Islamic countries and countries with large Muslim minorities. For instance, an Arabic entrepreneur may seek a Malaysian venture capitalist to start up a business. The *mushārakah* may be high risk but it focuses more on resource mobilisation, social justice and fair distribution of profit and resources. Although high risk, the profit is earned in a moderate manner and not based on speculation that would only increase the risk and losses of an investment.

The degree of losses from risk taking through a profit- and loss-sharing contract and speculation are totally different.

In a profit- and loss-sharing contract, losses are spread out and shared management provides a cushion for the parties involved in the investment. This encourages equity participation. In other words, what you invest and what you work for is what you obtain. The element of risk must be present. Based on the finance theory in the conventional economy, a higher risk always leads to a higher return. However, the future remains uncertain, as always, and therefore a higher risk also means high losses. This should not be a disadvantage simply because interest overburdens individuals and companies during the recessionary period because interest payment is an obligation. Frequency of the income is much better although in small amounts, rather than hoping and speculating to receive a bigger sum in one go. A level of moderateness is very much encouraged in Islam as Islam opposes extremism of any kind.

Equity finance provides a good platform for foreign equity capital, especially in developing countries. The exchange of technology, management skills and financial skills is vital in developing countries and with this avenue of financing it can help to build the economies of the developing countries through increases in employment and establishing small and strong businesses. This is the same technique used by the Mexican government through the 'maquiladora' programme. According to Aureliano Gonzalez Baz:

> Maquiladora is a Mexican Corporation which operates under a maquila program approved for it by the Mexican Secretariat of Commerce and Industrial Development (SECOFI). A maquila program entitles the company, first, to foreign investment participation in the capital and in management of up to 100% without need of any special authorization. Second, it entitles the company to special customs treatment, allowing duty free temporary import of machinery, equipment, parts and materials,

and administrative equipment such as computers, and communications devices, subject only to posting a bond guaranteeing that such goods will not remain in Mexico permanently. All of a maquiladora's products are exported, either directly, or indirectly, through sale to another maquiladora or exporters. The type of production may be the simple assembly of temporarily imported parts. The manufacture from start to finish of a product uses materials from various countries, including Mexico or any conceivable combination of the various phases involved in manufacturing, or even non-industrial operations, such as data-processing, packaging, and sorting coupons.[1]

The maquiladora provides a structure for foreign equity. This can be done through *Shari'ah* compliant private equity and Islamic venture capital. Every country has unique resources. Through foreign equity capital such resources can be equally manufactured and shared for the good of mankind. Other than that the tax system can be slowly structured in an Islamic way which will be fair for both parties that are involved. Furthermore, both parties involved share the risk.

The establishment of partnerships through joint venture or through venture capital financing will create an environment of financial policies following the guidelines of the *Shari'ah* principles and this will further motivate poorer Muslim countries to participate. The Islamic emphasis on the fulfilment of all contractual obligations would provide the confidence that foreign investors need. This, if achieved, will leave little room for fraudulent cases. It also helps to boost investment in the creation of new products and services. These new products and services would later on be exported and thus the country in question develops as one which supplies goods for export rather than just purchasing foreign goods.

SMEs are important as they can play a major role in establishing a *Shari'ah* compliant private equity and Islamic venture capital industry. In addition, they create new jobs, products and services. Poor Muslim countries have a big supply of labour but lack educational infrastructure for vocational and professional training. Therefore the SME can be an avenue for people to become employed or self-employed. In Italy, for example, artisans, who often work in family businesses, play an important role in the success of Italian jewellery, gold, silver, leatherworking, embroidery, glasswork, furniture, pottery, shoemaking, and cloth manufacturing.[2]

Every country has unique resources and with the existence of SMEs, these resources can be explored and used to their fullest extent for both domestic use and export. Apart from this, existing sectors available in the country can be further nurtured through research and development. SMEs are more labour intensive and in most countries they get help from the government. Equity financing through *Shari'ah* compliant private equity and Islamic venture capital can help to assist these small businesses to enter the market. Such financing is there not only as an investor or a fund provider but also to guide the business. New ideas and concepts can be developed and, when marketed successfully, help to increase the economy of a country. It may not have as great an impact as the larger industries, however with many small businesses it spurs competition and creativity and this helps to increase growth and performance in the company.

Regarding equity financing alleviating a country's poverty, the shared management feature in a profit- and loss-sharing contract in *Shari'ah* compliant private equity and Islamic venture capital is a good tool for strengthening brotherhood among Muslims and through entrepreneurship.

According to the rate of success of the business, this can also be on an international scale. Apart from this, the *zakat* paid by these small businesses can help to eradicate poverty within the area that the company is operating. If there are many smaller companies in the country, more *zakat* is paid. Another way in which the SME can overcome poverty is through the employment opportunities that it offers. Due to more people working it creates other demands and supplies that help shape the economy of a particular area. In response to more money flowing and more transactions at hand, plus the fair distribution of wealth through *zakat*, the problem of poverty can be overcome. Industries such as *Shari'ah* compliant private equity and Islamic venture capital through profit- and loss-sharing modes of financing can boost SMEs in other Islamic countries.

Financial instruments and their contracts operate with risk and uncertainty when used as a mode of financing in any business transaction. Equity and debt are commonly used as a mode of financing in venture capital investment. Debt can be used in the mezzanine and consolidation stages in private equity funding. The debt contracts as opposed to equity may increase the return on equity of a certain company, due to tax exemption of the interest. However, problems persist should the interest not be paid and the company may be filed for bankruptcy. Apart from this, regardless of the invested company's performance, there is still an obligation to pay the debt.

The difference between equity and debt lies in risk allocation, ownership rights, management and incentives. Equity financing is money raised by the business and provided by the venture capitalist in exchange for a share of ownership within a company. In equity financing, the business owners sell shares in their company for an agreed sum. However, debt financing is funds borrowed by the entrepreneur that need to be paid up front at a specific point in time, including the interest. Debt financing is normally used in the later stage of the company and can be issued on a long- or short-term basis.

Equity financing which uses instruments such as ordinary shares puts the investor in a risky position when the business fails. However, the investor has voting rights and manages the company. As for preference shares, shareholders do not get voting rights but receive fixed dividends. Some preference shares may be issued in the form of convertible preference shares, whereby they can be converted into ordinary shares. This type of preference shares is permissible in Islam and approved by *Shari'ah*. Preference shares help to protect the investors' share in the investment or the invested company should it take a downturn. Upon exiting from the invested company, the investors receieve capital gains from their shares. Debt holders, meanwhile, will benefit from the situation even though they do not manage the business. If a company uses debt, the return on equity for the company increases as compared to using just equity due to the tax shelter provided by interest and due to the high risk borne by the shareholders for using debt financing, placing them last on the list when company assets are liquidated due to bankruptcy.

When applying debt, financing and interest are not paid: it is considered a liability to the company, and again assets may be liquidated to pay off the interest. From the financier's side, debt looks more lucrative compared to equity financing because financiers do not hold high risk and still get a fixed return through interest without taking part in the business. From the entrepreneur's side debt is a burden because it is a financial obligation and a liability to the company. Equity would be more promising to the entrepreneur since ownership is shared with the financier, especially in the case of venture capital. In this case, both venture capitalist and the entrepreneur work together to increase the value of the capital provided by the venture capitalist. Table 5.1 compares debt with equity in a summary of the pros and cons.

Table 5.1 *Debt financing versus equity financing*

Debt financing	Equity financing
Interest repayment	Receive dividends
Need collateral	Do not need collateral
Debt providers are not risk takers; they just want to make sure that the interest is paid	Equity holders are risk takers as they have stakes in an investment that is tied to the investment performance
Do not have voting rights	Have voting rights
Interest is tax deductible	Dividends are not tax deductible
Loans need to be paid	Equity can be kept for long-term investment
Leveraged company's profit	Shareholders share the profit of the company

Profit- and loss-sharing concepts applied in Islamic venture capital and *Shari'ah* compliant private equity help to create economic wealth, in particular in the SME sector. Profit- and loss-sharing instruments aid companies at the start-up stage in terms of shared management and risks and in managing the business to create value for the investment. Shared management and risk can slowly eliminate the risk of the business and investment being unsuccessful. Cooperation via profit- and loss-sharing instruments through equity participation can boost the economy of developing countries by means of innovative ideas, which can create new markets and increase employment. Resources can be maximised in the most efficient way. In addition, poverty can be reduced through developing small businesses that can create employment.

5.2 Valuation methods for investments

A *Shari'ah* compliant private equity and Islamic venture capital fund must abide by Islamic accounting standards. Furthermore, from an Islamic perspective, there should be no price manipulation and price control in a transaction that results in a party being victimised. Pricing as a result of valuation is subject to uncertainty, such as cash flow analysis which depends on future cash flows.

In the venture capital industry where risk plays a major role in determining profit it is vital that there is a valuation method that reflects the true value of the invested company. The importance of this is to ensure that the valuation avoids *ghubn* and *gharar*. Also significant is the concept of *'iwad*, whereby the price paid by the consumer, or in this case the parties involved in the investment, should justify the return they are about to get from the purchase. The profit margin must be in line with *'iwad*. According to Ibn al-'Arabi, an influential Islamic philosopher, 'Every increase which is without *'iwad* or an equal counter value is *riba*.'[3]

Different industries may use different methods. The industry and the market of a specific investment play a crucial part because different industries may be subject to different valuation methods. The stage of the development of the company is also of importance because at the early stage the invested company does not have assets and the business is not established, therefore applying such valuation methods as the cash flow method may not be appropriate.

5.2.1 *Islamic accounting standard and AAOIFI*

One of the differences between Islamic accounting and conventional accounting is that Islamic accounting focuses on market price rather than historical cost. It also measures assets at saleable value. The objectives of Islamic financial accounting standards and reporting for the Islamic venture capital and *Shari'ah* compliant private equity industry is to ensure that it coincides with *Shari'ah* law. This includes transparency and accuracy. Reports should not be misleading and should include financial statements showing the Islamic venture capital and *Shari'ah* compliant private equity function as an investor or as the party managing the fund.

Financial statements include an income statement, a balance sheet, a statement of cash flow, as well as unrestricted investments and their equivalents. The unrestricted investments account is to disclose the profit and loss shared between the investor and the invested company or entrepreneur. The contractual relationship between the two must be disclosed as well. The statement on *zakat* calculation and its sources is also part of the financial statement. *Zakat* will be calculated based on the net assets that have depreciated and *zakat* in many cases are tax exempt. This can be beneficial for a company at the start-up stage. With regard to the financial statements based on *Shari'ah* standards, this will be followed by valuation on the invested company, which can be analysed through the following methods:

- price earnings multiple
- cash flow analysis

- net asset value
- liquidation value

5.2.2 *Price earnings multiple*

In general, a high price earnings multiple (P/E) suggests that investors are expecting higher earnings growth in the future compared to investments in companies with a lower P/E. However, the P/E ratio does not tell the whole story. It is usually more useful to compare the P/E ratios of one company to other companies in the same industry, to the market in general or against the company's own historical P/E. It would not be useful for investors using the P/E ratio to compare the P/E of companies in different industries due to different growth rates in each sector. P/E ratio or any other method of valuation is applicable in the early stage because there is not much cash in a company at the start-up stage and there is a risk of the company becoming bankrupt. However, this does not mean that it is not applicable at the later stage. It is realistic to use the P/E ratio as compared to other methods of valuation.

5.2.3 *Cash flow analysis*

Cash flow analysis is a valuation method used to estimate the attractiveness of an investment opportunity. Discounted cash flow (DCF) analysis uses future cash flow projections and discounts them using the weighted average cost of capital to arrive at a present value, which is then used to evaluate the potential of an investment. If the present value is positive, this means that the investment should be considered. Cash flow analysis is more appropriately applied in the later stages whereby the company is more established (has steady cash flows) and the value of the company can be forecasted. Cash flow analysis and the net asset value are more appropriately applied at the later stages whereby the business and the product have already developed.

5.2.4 Net asset value

Net asset value (NAV) is calculated as the total assets of a company minus the intangible assets such as goodwill, patents and trademarks, less all liabilities and the par value of preferred stock. It is also known as 'book value'. It is likely to be appropriate for a business whose value derives mainly from the underlying value of its assets rather than its earnings, such as property holding companies and investment businesses. NAV is only applicable to mature companies and listed companies. It can be applied in manufacturing companies and capital intensive companies. In the early stage, companies do not have many assets and therefore the NAV will not give the true value of the company. NAV valuation may not be the best method for early stage companies. The company starts with a high NAV and within months this reduces. Companies do not make revenue at this stage and therefore the NAV declines over time. The NAV is more appropriate for later stage companies where they have already acquired some assets and the net worth of these companies can be calculated.

5.2.5 Liquidation value

Trade sale involves selling shares to another potential buyer or another venture capital company. In some cases, the earnings obtained through trade sale are higher compared to those of the initial public offering (IPO). The potential buyer could expand the business into other countries and the value will increase. It shows that these two exit mechanisms provide high return.

It is hard to say if the diminishing *mushārakah* where the entrepreneur gradually buys out its stake from the venture capitalist can give a high return when compared to the IPO or the trade sale as preferred by the respondents. Buying back shares periodically and applying diminishing *mushārakah* as an exit mechanism is viable as long as the target returns are achieved and provide a platform for parties to maintain a win–win situation in the investment deal. The advantage of a share buyback, or the diminishing *mushārakah* for that matter, over the IPO, is that the entrepreneur is not tied up with reporting to the regulators and it would probably be less costly.

In relation to the IPO listing, the *Shari'ah* Advisory Council of the Securities Commission Malaysia currently conducts a *Shari'ah* compliance reviews process at the pre-IPO stage. In terms of *Shari'ah* compliance matters there is a regulator in Malaysia that can provide guidelines and consultations. For the other exit mechanisms the process is not as stringent when compared to that of an IPO.

5.3 Risk mitigation and management

The venture capital business is considered as a financing method that highlights transparency at the early stage of the business cycle. Board directors are appointed and invested companies are monitored. This encourages guided risk taking with knowledge of managing a business. Some of the biggest risks in the venture capital companies concern the management, market and return. Identifying the risk leads us to analyse further the risk mitigation procedures of *Shari'ah* compliant private equity funding and Islamic venture capital.

5.3.1 *Types of risk involved in* Shari'ah *compliant private equity funding*

In terms of management and risk, governance, trustworthiness, competency and credibility are to be considered. Management is an important criteria to be looked at before undertaking an investment. In terms of marketability and the success of products and services run by the invested company, it depends on the business climate, business viability, changes in technology, government policies and market trends. Business risk is one of the biggest risks in the venture capital industry.

For example, based on the Bank Negara Malaysia's annual report 2005, the sector that comprises the highest investment in the venture capital industry is the information and communication technology sector. Information and communication technology is a fast-paced sector and when the market dynamics change, the product and service may become irrelevant and out of place. In terms of return, venture capital companies are concerned about not obtaining the return on investment as the industry itself is very risky and the failure rate is high.

5.3.2 *Sharing of risks and management*

The venture capital company plays a major role in the risk management of the investments and also the investee companies. The entrepreneur manages the risk pertaining to the daily operations of the business and is responsible for the risk assessment, operations and strategic role of the company since the entrepreneur is running the business and created the business originally. This can be compared to *mushārakah* where risk and management are shared between the parties involved in the investment. This helps to increase trustworthiness and instil cooperation between the investor and the entrepreneur.

5.3.3 *Rights and responsibilities of the investors and entrepreneurs*

The venture capitalist and the private equity company holds the greatest responsibility in the risk management of the invested company from an investment perspective. The entrepreneur usually focuses on the daily operations of running the business and anything related to it.

The rights of the parties involved in the investment deal are important in a private equity and venture capital agreement. Furthermore, they enhance transparency in the agreements. The contract and agreements will cover the rights and responsibilities of both parties. The rights of investors and entrepreneurs cover areas such as transparency, corporate governance, risk management and financial objectives. These have to be nurtured at the early stages of the business and continued at the later stage. Apart from this, the responsibilities listed in the contract indicate what is promised by each party and that these promises must be executed.

The agreement binds all the rights and responsibilities of both parties. The rights and responsibilities that the venture capital and private equity companies have are part of their value-adding process in terms of the invested companies. The responsibility of venture capital companies is to ensure that the investee company moves in the direction mutually agreed upon and provides assistance. For example, those venture capital companies registered with the Securities Commission Malaysia must provide period reporting to the Securities Commission Malaysia such as an annual activity report for venture capital corporations (VCCs) and venture capital management corporations (VCMCs).[4] This must be submitted to the Securities Commission Malaysia within 30 days from each year-end. It should include information on the funds, actual investments in local and international venture companies (by business stage and by industry sectors) and information on the VCC/VCMCs' portfolio of venture companies. The company is encouraged to provide information on its performance during the year, problems and constraints encountered, future plans for development and views on the local and international venture capital industries. Audited financial statements are to be submitted within three months of the close of each financial year end.

This is to ensure good performance, governance and transparency of the venture capital companies. Information on the invested company is required as well. The venture capital company must ensure that the management of the investee and the invested company provides information that is accurate, clear, unambiguous, confidential and provided in a timely manner.

To structure a *Shari'ah* compliant private equity or Islamic venture capital fund, the agreement must be transparent regarding the rights and responsibilities of the venture capital companies and the invested company. Knowing the rights and responsibilities of the parties involved ensures fair distribution of profit, loss, management and risk. The rights and responsibilities of the partners in a *mushārakah* contract are set out in Table 5.2.

Table 5.2 *Rights and responsibilities of* mushārakah *partners.*

Rights	Responsibilities
• To borrow or lend.	• The prohibition of interest.
• To make transactions on credit.	• To ensure the investment/ business is halal.
• To give capital to a third party on a mudhārabah basis.	• The circulation of wealth through zakat payment.
• To give capital to a third party on a shirkah basis.	• The transparency of all contract and agreement and business transactions.
• To bring new partners to the partnership.	• To be efficient and to act as stated in the agreement.
• To enter into another new partnership in a private capacity.	• To assist each other during tough times.
	• Not to burden other partners with debt.

The rights and responsibilities of the *mushārakah* are the responsibility of the Securities Commission *Shari'ah* Advisory Council (SAC), lawyers (well versed in *Shari'ah* law and Islamic contracts), the venture capital company and the invested company. The *mushārakah* is flexible in listing the rights and responsibilities of the parties involved and not considering too much the structure of the business entity.

This takes us back to the flexibility of Islamic law as stated above in structuring a contract and as applied in an Islamic venture capital and a *Shari'ah* compliant private equity fund. This requires the contracts and the financial statements to be transparent and there is also a need for more *Shari'ah* lawyers to handle Islamic contracts as there may be many agreements involved which include the rights and responsibilities of the *Shari'ah* compliant private equity funding and the entrepreneur. The agreements are crucial to ensure a fair investment deal in a *Shari'ah* compliant private equity fund.

Discussing the benefits of profit and loss sharing instruments to wealth creation demonstrates the advantages and disadvantages of the *mushārakah* and *mudhārabah* in terms of valuation methods, risk mitigation, and the rights and responsibilities of parties involved in the investment deal. In *Shari'ah* compliant private equity and Islamic venture capital funding, such analysis and discussion is vital to avoid *ghubn* and *gharar*. It also helps find the optimum financing method for the *Shari'ah* compliant private equity and Islamic venture funding where it can create value to the investment deal.

5.4 Case studies

5.4.1 *Asia:* Mushārakah *in Malaysia*
Mushārakah in Malaysia in the area of venture capital is still in its infancy. Although Commerce International Merchant

Bankers Bhd (CIMB) structured the CIMB Muamalat Fund 1, which is a *Shari'ah* compliant fund, there is still room for other venture capital in Malaysia to take the same step. A US$50 million venture capital fund was launched by the Islamic Development Bank (IDB), targeting high-tech ventures in Muslim countries. Census results from 2005 show that there were 518,996 SMEs, representing 99.2 per cent of total business establishments in Malaysia, while large enterprises (LEs) consisted of 4,136 business establishments in Malaysia.[5] There were 411,849 micro-enterprises, making up 74.9 per cent of the total number of SMEs and 78.7 per cent of overall business in Malaysia.[6] According to the census, the majority of SMEs are concentrated in agriculture, manufacturing and services.[7]

The SME can become an excellent platform to engineer financing through Islamic venture capital or *mushārakah* funds for *halal* businesses. The above examples show us that the potential for *mushārakah* funds in a venture capital or as a financial institution is huge, especially with the emergence of the *halal* food industry and for other industries as well. Malaysia can establish partnerships with other Muslim countries. According to K. Salman Younis, managing director of Kuwait Finance House (Malaysia) Berhad,

> *Mushārakah* is definitely one of the most effective ways which can be used to help drive the *halal* industry in Malaysia and other countries. However, the success of this form of financing also depends on the Islamic banking community having the expertise in the *halal* business.[8]

According to Mohamad Safri Shahul Hamid of CIMB Islamic, '*Mushārakah* is one of the four approved *Shari'ah* principles together with *isti'na*, *ijarah* and *mudharabah* – that provide certain tax (Malaysian) benefits to the issuer.'[9]

In the banking sector, *mushārakah* is also used as a financing tool in most Islamic banks that offer Islamic banking products. However, *mushārakah* does not appeal much to the banks due to the mismatch of maturities of the assets and liabilities in the banks' balance sheets and the resulting liquidity risk. In addition, moral hazard and information asymmetry also make *mushārakah* financing less attractive to the Islamic banks. Furthermore, banks just provide the funds and do not take part in the management, but in a *mushārakah* the parties involved must take part in the management of the business or the investment.

Malaysia introduced its first Islamic venture capital fund, of RM35 million, in 2008. The fund is managed by Mushārakah Venture Management. Malaysia, supported by the government, is putting its utmost effort into developing the venture capital industry with funds mostly invested at the early stage and expansion/growth stage.

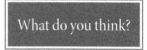

1. How does the infrastructure in Malaysia assist in developing Islamic venture capital?
2. What are the risks involved in Islamic venture capital in relation to a *mushārakah* contract?
3. What valuation method would be appropriate for an Islamic venture capital fund?

5.4.2 *MENA: Infrastructure funds and Islamic private equity development*

The Bahrain Ithmar Bank and Dubai-based Abraaj Capital raised a US$2 billion Islamic private equity fund to invest in infrastructure in the Middle East, North Africa and

South Asia.[10] The Islamic private equity funds established by Bahrain Ithmar Bank and Dubai-based Abraaj Capital are structured to meet the regional demand for private equity investments.[11] This is a big advantage for the private equity companies in MENA. Another example is the Dhow Gulf Opportunities Fund launched by Qatar Islamic Bank – a US$1 billion fund which focuses on telecoms, environmental recycling technologies, media, oil and gas, and infrastructure.[12] Dubai International Capital Emerging Markets along with HSBC Bank Middle East Ltd (HSBC) and Oasis International Leasing PJSC (Oasis) in Abu Dhabi established the MENA Infrastructure Fund LP (MENA IF), a US$500 million fund targeting investment opportunities in infrastructure projects in the Middle East and North Africa.[13] The spending for infrastructure is high and the figures are increasing each year.

Following the MENA Infrastructure Fund, Oasis International Leasing (OASIS) of Abu Dhabi also agreed to sponsor the US$500 million fund.[14] Public–private partnership is used in developing the infrastructure.

> The MENA Infrastructure Fund was launched in March 2006. It has a broad mandate to invest in infrastructure development such as utilities, energy, transportation and public private partnership. The fund will invest in both project companies and other entities wishing to expand their infrastructure operations in the region.[15]

The large pool of infrastructure funds is definitely a source for developing the *Shari'ah* compliant private equity industry in the MENA region. Furthermore, the sectors covered by the infrastructure funds will spur innovation in products and services that can benefit mankind.

What do you think?

1. How does the infrastructure fund assist in developing Islamic private equity in the MENA region?
2. What are the risks involved with regard to investments through shareholder-subordinated loan stock? Is it *Shari'ah* compliant?
3. Would the infrastructure funds be a good platform for establishing Islamic venture capital or *Shari'ah* compliant private equity funding?

5.4.3 *The United Kingdom and Europe: Islamic LBO – innovation in Islamic investment banking*

The European financial system has always proven its efficacy in providing services and financial solutions to create a profitable investment. One example is the buyout of Aston Martin using Islamic LBO. West LB assisted the syndication of the largest Islamic LBO in the United Kingdom. The buyout was backed by two GCC firms, Adeem Investment and Investment Dar, to the amount of US$522 million. Although the buyout looks lucrative, there are challenges in the procedures.

Toby Lewis, in 'West LB syndicates US$225 million of Islamic Aston Martin Debt', writes that 'the hybrid deal had been difficult to structure, as the UK tax law raises complexities for Islamic finance.' In the same article, Harvey Hoogakker of West LB states that 'the underlying asset is a UK based asset and not all techniques in the GCC sit well with the legislation in the UK'. Another important point highlighted in the same article is that 'the debt has been sold over an eight year period, with a "put option" after five years to entice holders tentative about investing in an innovative Islamic structure'.[16]

There are other deals in the UK financed by Islamic LBO aside from Aston Martin. One example is Amtech Power Software. Both examples show that Islamic finance is making its way to another phase where financial engineering takes place. Financial instruments used in Islamic finance should be able to address the most complex financial situation, other than making it *Shari'ah* compliant only.

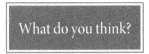

1. What are the prospects for Islamic LBOs in the United Kingdom?
2. Does an Islamic LBO create value more than the conventional LBO?
3. What are the challenges faced in structuring hybrid deals in Islamic private equity?
4. How is profit- and loss-sharing applied in an Islamic LBO?

5.4.4 North America: Legal challenges in structuring the profit- and loss-sharing rule in private equity and venture capital funding

The growing population of Muslims in the United States has increased demand for *Shari'ah* compliant products such as Islamic insurance, Islamic retail banking products (home financing), Islamic unit trusts, and Islamic venture capital and *Shari'ah* compliant private equity funding. One of the challenges when structuring Islamic venture capital and *Shari'ah* compliant private equity funding is the application of the profit- and loss-sharing rule to the investment deal. The knowledge and willingness of the parties involved are also crucial for a smooth investment deal procedure because both venture capitalist and investee company are on the same level.

According to Umar F. Moghul, in his article 'American Islamic private equity transactions: Successes, challenges and opportunities' in which he explores a recently closed transaction involving an investment bank investing in a US consumer goods business:

> Most Islamic private equity transactions in the US have simply done away with the concept of profit–loss sharing and in so doing, we have learned that some conventional investors may actually prefer the absence of such preference because they believe it results in greater equality among shareholders and incentivises parties who might otherwise be positioned more adversely.[17]

This demonstrates the advantages of applying profit–loss sharing in an investment deal and how it benefits the parties involved. At some point the preference shares give a better investment cushion to the venture capitalist as compared to the target company. In relation to the valuation method, Umar F. Moghul states in the same article that the investment deal articulated redemptions and dividends in a manner reflective of the market value and performance of the company, which is very much abiding by *Shari'ah* compliancy guidelines.[18]

What do you think?

1. Which valuation method would be appropriate in this case study? (For example, P/E multiple, NAV, cash flow technique.)

2. Using ordinary shares gives more advantages to the target companies in a private equity fund. Is this correct?
3. What are the prospects for structuring Islamic private equity and Islamic venture capital in the US?
4. Would the profit–loss sharing instruments or contracts be just as competitive in the conventional market?

Notes

1. Aureliano Gonzalez Baz, 'What is a maquiladora?' (n.d.), http://www.udel.edu/leipzig/texts2/vox128.htm (retrieved 7 November 2010).
2. Alan Friedman, 'Italian small business: the backbone of the economy explored', *Financial Times*, 15 September 1987, p. 1.
3. Saiful Azhar, *Critical Issues on Islamic Banking and Financial Markets: Islamic Economics, Banking and Finance, Investments, Takaful and Financial Planning* (Kuala Lumpur: Dinamas, 2005), pp. 30–3.
4. Securities Commission Malaysia (n.d.), http://www.sc.com. my/eng/html/licensing/vencapregkit.html (retrieved 10 April 2010).
5. *Status and Performance of Small and Medium Enterprises*, 2005, http://www.bnm.gov.my/files/publication/sme/en/ 2005/chap_2.pdf (retrieved 15 February 2010).
6. Ibid.
7. Ibid.
8. *The Halal Journal*, June 2006, http://www.halaljournal.com/ artman/publish_php/article_1005.php (retrieved 8 November 2009).
9. Ibid.
10. 'New MENA infrastructure fund launches', *Trade Finance*, June 2006, vol. 9, no. 5, p. 12.
11. Ibid.
12. Paul McNamara, 'Islamic investment banking 2009', Yassar Media.

13. Dubai International Capital: MENA Infrastructure Fund, http://www.dubaiic.com/en/default/mena-infrastructure-fund.html (retrieved 4 March 2010).
14. 'MENA Infrastructure Fund expands ownership base', 27 September 2006, http://www.ameinfo.com/97594 (retrieved 12 December 2009).
15. Ibid.
16. Toby Lewis, 'West LB syndicates US$225 million of Islamic Aston Martin debt', http://www.privateequityonline.com/Article.aspx?article=13569&hashID=8817E854DAC861C223F70CFA1E036CFB73FAD345 (retrieved 7 May 2010).
17. Umar F. Moghul, 'American Islamic private equity transactions: Successes, challenges and opportunities', http://www.eurekahedge.com/news/07_july_IFN_American_Islamic_PE_Transactions_Successes_Challenges_and_Opportunities.asp (retrieved 5 December 2010).
18. Ibid.

CHAPTER 6

EXIT STRATEGIES AND FINANCIAL STRUCTURE

Choosing the most appropriate financial structure and exit strategy for an investment is not a straightforward task. There are many financial instruments available in the industry but which one will provide a high return and add value to the investment for a *Shariʻah* compliant private equity or venture capital company? Which exit strategy is most appropriate for the investment taken in order to get a higher return on investment? This depends on many factors such as the timing of the exit, the stage of funding and cost. Nevertheless, the most important matter is to ensure the decision taken will benefit both the investor and the invested company whereby the risk and reward is fairly distributed between both parties. This is the feature of a profit- and loss-sharing structure which is applied in a *Shariʻah* compliant fund, be it in private equity or venture capital.

6.1 Financial instruments for *Shariʻah* compliant funds

Discussion of financial instruments is not just based on their *Shariʻah* compliancy but also on factors such as the stage of funding and value for money for the investment. The instruments are analysed here in terms of their financial advantages and disadvantages for the investor and invested company.

6.1.1 *Preferred stocks*

Convertible preferred equity is more likely to be used with seed and early stage investments and with firms in the internet and communications sectors (in the Malaysia venture capital industry). Preferred stocks provide a risk management element and are more appropriate in the early stages. Ordinary shares are more appropriate in the later stages. Ordinary shareholders can get returns through capital gains in mature companies at the later stage. Ordinary shares are easier to manage and do not need to go through capital reduction and many legal procedures. Preference shares are likely to be used in early stages and ordinary shares in the later stages.

In venture capital, preference shares can be exercised later through redeemable cumulative preference shares and redeemable preference shares. Preference shares have to be used for venture capital exit avenues where redemption and conversion takes place. Preference shares give their holders a right to a fixed dividend but they do not have voting rights. Preference shares may be issued with the right of conversion into ordinary shares, where they are called convertibles. Listed below are some examples of the types of preference share:

- **Convertible preferred shares.** Preferred stock that includes an option for the holder to convert the preferred shares into a fixed number of common shares, usually any time after a pre-determined date.
- **Cumulative redeemable convertible preference shares.** A type of share whereby the invested company buys back its shares by exercising its call options. The venture

capitalist exercises their put options at the redemption date.

- **Redeemable preference shares.** A type of preference share whereby the issuing company has the right to redeem. This preference share may not necessarily have a redemption date.
- **Cumulative preference shares.** If the company fails to pay the dividend to the holders, this preferred stock provides the holders with an entitlement to receive dividends at the next declaration date. The preference shareholders have the right to receive their dividends first, before an ordinary shareholder. It is cumulative and is subject to the amount of cash available in the company.
- **Participating preferred share.** 'A type of preferred stock that under certain conditions gives holders the right to receive earnings payouts over and above the specified dividend rate.'[1]

The *Shari'ah* Advisory Council (SAC) of the Securities Commission in Malaysia resolved that as of 14 July 1999, basic preference shares (non-cumulative) are permissible based on *tanazul*.[2] *Tanazul* means to drop entitlements to right. The Companies Act 1965 defined a preference share as a share that does not give a right to the preference shareholders to vote at a general meeting or any right to participate in any distribution of the company that has stated the amount, whether through dividends or redemption, dissolution or otherwise.[3] The SAC analysed that non-cumulative preference shares have a permanent holding period by the investors which is similar to that of the ordinary shareholders.[4] The dividends for the non-cumulative preference shares are fixed and non-cumulative. In addition, a non-cumulative preference share has no maturity date, similar to ordinary shares.

The SAC ruled that non-cumulative preference shares are permissible based on tanazul where the right to profit of the ordinary shareholder is given willingly to a preference shareholder. Tanazul is agreed upon at an annual general meeting of a company, which decides to issue preference shares in an effort to raise new capital. As it is agreed at the meeting to issue preference shares, this means that ordinary shareholders have agreed to give priority to preference shareholders in dividing the profits, in accordance with tanazul. In the context of preference share tanazul means surrendering the rights to a share of profit based on partnership, by giving priority to preference shareholders.[5]

Based on this explanation from the SAC, convertible preference shares and redeemable preference shares operate similarly to those of non-cumulative preference shares, whereby it is permissible based on *tanazul*. In this case, the venture capital buys the convertible preference shares from the invested company surrendering the rights to a share of profit based on partnership, by giving priority to preference shareholders. Participating and cumulative preference shares of any kind are not mentioned as *Shari'ah* permissible. As stated by the SAC, non-cumulative is permissible while cumulative is not mentioned. However, it is convertible. In a venture capital setting, participating preferred shares somehow allow the investor to receive profit twice from the face value of their investments and hold their equity ownership in a company. If this is the case, then the investors do not actually accept risk or practise correctly the risk-sharing concept as in the *mushārakah* contract. This may not be fair for the entrepreneur.

To summarise, convertible preference shares and redeemable preference shares operate similarly to those of non-cumulative preference shares, whereby they are permissible based on *tanazul*. Apart from this, using the appropriate instruments depends highly on the investment stage and on ordinary shares perhaps being more appropriate in the leveraged buyout at a later stage rather than in a start-up stage. There are several instruments that are *Shari'ah*, which are convertible preference shares and redeemable preference shares which can be used to structure an Islamic venture capital fund. Preference shares can also be used to structure an Islamic venture capital fund. Some of the advantages of using preference shares for a *Shari'ah* compliant fund are as follows:

- It is convertible and does not have preference shares surplus.
- It gives the right to claim before the ordinary shareholder upon liquidation.
- It provides a better platform for the invested company to exit because the preference shares can be converted into ordinary shares and redeemed.
- The preference shareholders receive dividend payments.
- It provides minimal risk exposure in business risk.
- It is practical at the start-up stage where the business risk is high.

To put this into perspective, a newly established company, FM Ltd, is looking for funding from an Islamic venture capital company, RK Ltd. After going through the FM Ltd business plan, RK Ltd decides to provide funding of £7 million. They both agree that the business plan should materialise by the next round of funding. RK Ltd valued FM Ltd at £12 million based on their financial standing. A profit-sharing deal is then agreed of 60 per cent shareholding by FM Ltd as the main shareholder and RK Ltd holds the remaining 40 per cent. After the deal is completed, a company called IK

Ltd wants to acquire FM Ltd at an offer of £10 million. FM Ltd agrees with the offer proposed by IK Ltd and earns a profit of £6 million. RK Ltd loses £3 million of the £7 million investment in FM Ltd.

Obviously this is a simple example and in real businesses the venture capitalist will protect its investment from such disastrous events. Financial instruments that can be used to protect investments are preferred stocks. Using the appropriate instruments depends on the investment stage as well. In the example above, if RK Ltd uses preferred stock it can redeem its original investment through redemption of the preferred shares. If RK Ltd had used redeemable preference shares with a face value of £7 million with a profit-sharing ratio of 60 per cent holding by FM Ltd and 40 per cent by RK Ltd, RK Ltd would have redeemed the preference shares at the face value of £7 million and the remaining £3 million would have been shared 1.8 million to FM Ltd and 1.2 million to RK Ltd. RK Ltd would have received back its original investment in this case.

However, it may not necessarily be a fair deal for the invested company, which in this example is FM Ltd, since applying profit- and loss-sharing instruments in the *Shari'ah* compliant fund is to ensure a fair degree of profit and risk distribution between the venture capital and the invested company. However, if convertible preference shares had been used and the offer was higher at a price of £20 million, RK Ltd would have converted its preference shares with a profit of £8 million.

6.1.2 *Common stocks*

Finding the right instrument for an investment deal is also important for ensuring that both parties get a fair return from the investment. It is vital to look for an instrument that gives fair profit-sharing for all parties involved in private

equity or venture capital funding. It is not as straightforward to apply the appropriate instrument for a *Shari'ah*
compliant fund as it depends on the size of the funding or
the shareholding and the type of business that had been
invested in as well as the exit strategy. It also has to be practical in the sense that it guarantees return on capital and is
financially efficient for all the parties involved in the investment. In the case of a *Shari'ah* compliant private equity
fund, ordinary shares which are *Shari'ah* compliant can be
an alternative. For a *Shari'ah* compliant private equity fund
ordinary shares may be applicable because at the later stage
it is not that risky for companies not to succeed as compared to the earlier stage. In general, factors for using ordinary shares also depend on the company's risk profile, value
for money, exit strategy, timing of the exit and legal cost.

Using the appropriate instruments depends on the
investment stage. Ordinary shares may be more appropriate in the leveraged buyout rather than in stages of venture capital. Convertible preferred equity is more likely to
be used with seed and early stage investments. Common
equity is used more often for expansion stage investments.
Preference shares provide a risk management element.
Preference shares protect investors by giving them the
right to claim assets first upon liquidation as compared to
ordinary shareholders. This is more practical at the early
stages whereby business risk is high. In the case of *Shari'ah*
compliant private equity and Islamic venture capital, the
convertible preferred equity is permissible and at the early
stage the investors do not have a high percentage ownership
using the convertible preference share.

The best exit strategy in this case would be the IPO or the
diminishing *mushārakah* for an Islamic venture capital and
ordinary shares for *Shari'ah* compliant private equity funding. In the exit avenue (IPO and diminishing *mushārakah*)

the preference shares would be converted to ordinary shares at a higher price where capital gains will be obtained by the investors. The legal cost is to be taken into consideration and also the cost efficiency of using the financial instrument for the funding.

6.1.3 *Hybrid securities*

- **Loan stocks.** Stocks act as collateral in the loan stock. The amount one can borrow depends on the value of the stocks. The loan earns a fixed interest rate similar to that of a standard loan. In this case, the loan stock is not *Shari'ah* compliant due to its interest bearing feature, and therefore it is not applicable in a *Shari'ah* compliant fund.
- **Irredeemable convertible unsecured loan stocks (ICULS).** This type of loan stock is similar to a warrant. It has a conversion ratio and can be converted into equity. The price of the stock depends on the conversion ratio. Holders of the ICULS are paid coupons at a pre-determined rate.

6.1.4 *Islamic private debt for leveraged buyouts*

The consolidation stage focuses on leveraged buyout funds and buys and builds strategies. According to David Gladstone and Laura Gladstone:

> In an independently owned small business, a leveraged buyout occurs when a non-owner management team buys the company from the original owners. Any of these situations is called a leveraged buyout or LBO because most of the money is invested into the company as debt.[6]

Buyout capital or LBO purchases the company together with the existing management using borrowed money. One of the first ever Islamic LBOs was the buyout of Aston Martin from Ford. The financiers for the deal were two Middle

East investment companies, Investment Dar and Adeem Investment Company. The *Shariʻah* compliant structure that was applied in this case was a *murabaha* commodity structure, where it is based on a profit- and loss-sharing mode of financing. This has paved the way for Islamic finance to enter into the private equity industry. For example, there is development and growth in *Shariʻah* compliant private equity funding in the Middle East. Table 6.1 shows the leading Gulf-based private equity funds.

Table 6.1 *Leading Gulf-based private equity funds*

Location	Company	Conventional or with *Shariʻah* board
Bahrain	Arcapita	Conventional
Bahrain	Investcorp	Conventional
Doha	Corecap	*Shariʻah* board
Dubai	Abrajj Capital	Conventional
Dubai	Millennium Private Equity	*Shariʻah* board
Dubai	Shuaa Capital	*Shariʻah* board
Kuwait	Gulf Finance House	Conventional
Kuwait	Investment Dar	*Shariʻah* board
Kuwait	NBK Capital	Conventional
Riyadh	Swicorp	Appointing *Shariʻah* board

Source: Rodney Wilson, 2009.[7]

The CIMB Group, Malaysia's largest investment bank, which includes CIMB Islamic, has a private equity subsidiary. CIMB focuses on medium- and long-term investments, often for five years or more. For regional investment CIMB has tied up with Navis Capital Partners, which has offices in Thailand, Hong Kong, India, Australia and Singapore, as well as Kuala Lumpur. Navis's holdings include vehicle components, car rental companies, logistics firms, catering operations and media ventures, most of which are *Shari'ah* compliant.[8]

However, the application of Islamic bonds or *sukuk* in the private equity sector, especially at the consolidation stage where companies are acquired through LBOs, still remains non-existent. The use of Islamic bonds or *sukuk* for LBOs is not that apparent, especially high yield ones, and further development is expected to be seen in the future.[9] This will motivate the key players in this industry to further engineer other Islamic financial instruments that can be used in the private equity and venture capital sectors. Given the insurmountable wealth in the Middle East and investment opportunities in South East Asia, mainly Malaysia and Singapore, *Shari'ah* based private equity funds can find their place in the consolidation stage of the private equity industry. This gives opportunites for investors to structure their funds in a *Shari'ah* compliant manner, especially at the consolidation stage where the focus is on leveraged buyout funds which involve high yield bonds plus buy and build strategies.

The importance of having *Shari'ah* compliant private equity for a leveraged buyout is not only for increasing opportunities to market and to structure a *Shari'ah* compliant fund in the private equity sector, but also to boost the small- and medium-sized enterprise (SME) sector in developing countries and emerging-economy countries where it will give them the choice between applying a *Shari'ah* compliant fund and a conventional one to buy out companies. However, there are many factors that must be taken into consideration when applying Islamic bonds to LBOs. For example, the value of the company, current market conditions, industry growth, exit mechanism performance, marketability, infrastructure, and legal issues are also of concern. Below are examples of the types of Islamic bond for financing LBOs:

- *murabaha*
- *ijarah*
- *mushārakah*
- *salam istisna*

Some of the advantages of using an Islamic LBO in private equity deals are due to its profitability and risk-sharing elements. It is also significant in certain industries, for example agriculture and manufacturing, where this is evident in SMEs in developing countries. In addition, it is based on equity sharing and an Islamic LBO does not depend on debt only, while only 33.3 per cent of debt is allowed in an Islamic LBO.

6.2 Potential exit strategies for a *Shariʿah* compliant private equity and Islamic venture capital fund

Investors do not want to keep an invested company in their portfolio forever and depending on the investment focus and strategy of the venture firm, they will seek to exit the investment in the portfolio company. The skill of the venture and private equity firm in successfully exiting its investment will determine the success of the exit for the venture capitalist and the entrepreneur. Below are several exit strategies applied in the venture capital industry.

6.2.1 *Initial public offering*
This is the first sale of stock by a company to the public. A company can raise money by issuing either debt (bonds) or equity. If the company has never issued equity to the public, it is known as an initial public offering (IPO).[10] It is quite time consuming for a company to prepare the company for an IPO. The invested company must have a board of

directors, audited financial accounts, lawyers, consultants, and so on. Most important are the underwriters: investment banks or merchant banks responsible for setting up the price of the share of the invested company and setting up a prospectus for the potential investors.

The process will also be reviewed by the Securities Commission to see if the regulations are adhered to. The companies and venture capitalists go for listing because they can sell their shares at a higher price as compared to a private placement. IPO allows the entrepreneur and the venture capitalist to sell the shares at a higher price in the public market. In this strategy a company needs to be transparent, as they have to provide information to their shareholders such as audited annual reports. When using IPO as a preferred exit strategy for Islamic venture capital:

- It enables the venture capital company to own shares
- It can generate high return on the investment
- It is attractive to the investors as they obtain dividends
- It is a good way to raise capital
- It can increase liquidity for the invested company
- It provides a potential exit strategy at the early stage.

The exit strategy also depends on the tenure of the investment and the business sector of the investment. In a short-term investment the choice is a put option, while in a long-term investment the choice is an IPO. In relation to the IPO listing, the SAC of the Securities Commission Malaysia currently conducts *Shari'ah* compliance reviews at the pre-IPO stage. In terms of *Shari'ah* compliance in Malaysia, there is a regulator in Malaysia that can provide guidelines and consultations. This is important for a *Shari'ah* compliant private equity fund or an Islamic venture capital fund whereby the processes have to abide by *Shari'ah* guidelines.

The establishment of the Malaysian Exchange of Securities Dealing and Automated Quotation (MESDAQ) provided a viable exit mechanism for investee companies in Malaysia. The objective of the MESDAQ is to provide a platform for high-growth companies to raise capital and promote technology industries and assist in developing a science and technology base for Malaysia through indigenous research development.[11] Table 6.2 shows IPO listings through the MESDAQ market in Malaysia. The number of listings demonstrates the important role played by the MESDAQ market with regard to the venture capital companies and invested companies.

Table 6.2 *Listed companies in Malaysia as at 13 April 2007*

Year	Main board	Second board	MESDAQ market	Total
2007	645	245	130	1020
2006	649	250	128	1027
2005	646	268	107	1021
2004	622	278	63	963
2003	598	276	32	906
2002	562	294	12	868

Source: Bursa Malaysia.[12]

6.2.2 *Management buyout (MBO)*

Managers and/or executives of a company purchase a controlling interest in a company from existing shareholders.[13] This method requires a willing seller. Typical reasons for the purchase of a business by its existing management include:

- Certain parts of an organisation are no longer seen as a core competence or there is no core activity by its parent company.

- A company is in financial distress and 'needs the cash'.
- Parts of acquisitions are not wanted.
- In the case of a family business: succession issues through retirement of the owner.
- The management team stands to gain independence and autonomy, a chance to influence the strategy and future direction of the company and the prospect of a capital gain.[14]

A management buyout (MBO) may be attractive to a seller for the following reasons:

- Speed. An MBO can be much quicker than a trade sale.
- Strategic considerations. For example, the selling party may not wish competitors to acquire control.
- Confidentiality. The selling party may not wish to let competitors have access to sensitive information that would be disclosed during a trade sale process.
- Familiarity. With an MBO the selling party can continue to deal with a management team with whom it has an established relationship.
- Pricing.[15]

Another exit strategy for an MBO is through puts and calls. The put option gives the venture capitalist the right to buy the company's share and the call option is the right for the company to buy the venture capitalist's shares at a predetermined formula. These formulas and valuations are based on the price/earnings ratio, net asset value and cash flow analysis.

This type of exit takes place when the managers and/or executives of a company purchase controlling interest in a company from existing shareholders.[16] The advantages of an MBO are that the entrepreneur is not tied up with reporting to the regulators and that it would probably be less costly when compared to an IPO. In addition, MBO would be a suitable exit strategy if the only financial instruments used in the investment deals are ordinary shares.

6.2.3 Management buy-in (MBI)

This happens when a group of investors outside a company purchases a controlling block of shares and then either keeps the existing management, or brings in new management.[17] The investors involved in the MBI believe that the company and its current management are of great value. A few representatives from the group of investors will usually be appointed to the company's board of directors.[18] The investor in this case may add value in terms of marketing the product or services and industry outlook. In some cases, the new investor may be another venture capitalist and can prepare the company for listing. Venture capitalists look upon sector experience and skills as being important for an MBI potential candidate to make sure that they understand the business and are reliable and credible, and to build a new solid relationship with the new management team.

6.2.4 Trade sale

Trade sale involves selling shares to another potential buyer or another venture capital company. In some cases, the earnings obtained through trade sale are higher compared to that of the IPO. The potential buyer could expand the business and the net worth will increase.

6.2.5 Mergers and acquisitions

A merger is a combination of two companies to form a new company while an acquisition is the purchasing of one company by another with no new company being formed.[19] Negotiating with the company to merge or acquire depends on how slow or fast the deal can be structured. In some cases, due to bureaucracy, the process can be very slow. Apart from this, the valuation of the company if it were to use different formulas and techniques may result in a bad deal for the company and the venture capitalist. However, if the acquiring company has a good track record and is well established, the synergistic benefits would be to the advantage of the invested company and venture capitalist whose stake still exists in the invested company.

6.3 Economic conditions and financial infrastructure for a successful company exit

6.3.1 *Advantages and disadvantages of profit-sharing and loss instruments*

The agreements of profit-sharing and loss instruments such as the *mushārakah* and *mudhārabah* can provide incentives for good behaviour among the parties involved, simply because the stringent agreements give them no opportunity to be dishonest. If any one of the parties involved goes against the agreement, a court order will be brought against that party. The efficient monitoring process carried out in venture capital and private equity assists in ensuring that the entrepreneur delivers as promised and strengthens the trust, relationship and value-adding between the two. Therefore, if the profit-sharing and loss instruments such as the *mushārakah* and *mudhārabah* are applied in the venture capital and private equity setting it only enriches the fund, not only as a fair pricing instrument, but also as one that provides incentives for good behaviour.

Asymmetric information may not be a major problem for profit-sharing and loss instruments in the venture capital and private equity setting as compared to the banks. In the venture capital industry, there are ways to minimise asymmetric information and moral hazard. First, the numerous agreements available help to manage asymmetric information, thus enhancing transparency from the early stages of the business and providing a good platform for a *Shari'ah* compliant fund. It spells out the rights and responsibilities for both the venture capitalist and the entrepreneur. Rodney Wilson argues that there is a higher level of trust between Islamic banks and their clients than in the case of conventional banks and hence the moral hazard is less.[20] If this is applied to the *Shari'ah* compliant fund it will definitely be an advantage to its establishment in Islamic venture capital and *Shari'ah* compliant private equity. He also suggests that higher levels of trust reduce risk and uncertainty, which in turn results in lower monitoring costs for Islamic banks.[21]

The management and profit- and loss-sharing features in the *mushārakah* provide efficient risk allocation and use of capital as a medium of financing on the equity side. This makes it ideal to be structured in the Islamic venture capital setting where equity financing is used to finance companies at the venture capital stage (early stage and the expansion stage). This is important because the investment stage plays a part in determining the instruments used as well as the valuation and exit strategy for the invested company. At this stage where it is highly risky, the financial instruments applied are important for profit distribution and determining exit strategy.

In terms of contracts, Islamic law states that determining liability is not based on the business structure, but on the actual *shirkah* contracts between the parties involved. If the parties want limited liability, they can choose *shirkah al'inan* or *mudhārabah* and if they want unlimited liability, they can choose *shirkah al-mufawadah*. This shows that there is potential to further expand contracts based on Islamic law to be used for a *mushārakah* fund in the venture capital setting. Issues in *mushārakah* arise at the point where it is applied. In the banking sector moral hazard and information asymmetry become a concern since the fund provider in this case does not conduct monitoring on the investments or the invested company as done by the venture capitalist. The nature of a bank's operation is mainly to act as a fund provider and not to operate like a venture capitalist. Since the banks may have shares in these invested companies they may have to appoint a special unit to monitor them.

This may incur extra cost to the banks. Other than this, the *mushārakah* is exposed to increased risk and is less liquid since it is asset backed, and the bank requires higher liquidity and reserves. This affects the reserve ratio of the bank, which is not a bad thing but the calculation is done differently. This extra risk may be transferred to the depositors as well, since the profit from the investment is shared with the depositors.

Another issue concerns the valuation of asset for the *mushārakah*. It is long-term financing and its valuation may be subject to inaccuracy. In the case of Islamic private debt securities and the *sukuk*, applying *mushārakah* or any other concept, such as *mudhārabah*, *ijarah* and *istisna*, issues are raised regarding accounting and valuation. This is due to differences in relation to the conventional accounting standards. The jurists of the *Malīkī* School have placed trading assets into three categories:[22]

- assets that are meant for buying and selling
- assets that are held for sale in the expectation of making profits through price appreciation in the future, and
- assets acquired for trade and not personal use

However, in the conventional classification of investment securities, it is classified into two types: dealing (short term); or investment (long term).[23] If we look at the classification that is outlined by the *Mālikī* jurists, it is more elaborate on its application while the conventional classification focuses on the investment from a business perspective only. The difference in terms of classification raises other issues in the area of valuation.

Another important section to be considered is in the legal area. If there is no merging between the Islamic law and the conventional, this becomes even more troublesome should there be fraudulent cases and there is no law to fall back on. The legal aspects of Islamic financial products and cases pertaining to them need continuous process and proper documentation for further reference.

6.3.2 *Diminishing* mushārakah

Diminishing *mushārakah* is a type of *mushārakah* that operates through the buyout of shares by the investors in the joint venture until the company is fully owned by the invested company. However, the buyout must result in a premium to the investors. The profit ratio will reduce as the shares of the parties or companies reduce through the share buyouts. The same concept is also applied in home

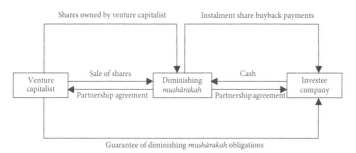

Figure 6.1 *Diminishing* mushārakah *exit mechanism*

financing. The structure of this type of *mushārakah* as an exit strategy is shown in Figure 6.1

The diminishing *mushārakah* is also structured by some banks for home financing. For example, Amanah Home Finance by the HSBC Amanah Finance is based on the diminishing *mushārakah* mode of financing. The first Islamic PDS issued in Malaysia was in 1990 by Shell MDS Sdn. Bhd. A syndicate of financiers arranged the *bai bithaman ajil* or BBA transaction of RM75 million for a tenure of five years and another RM50 million for a tenure of eight years. This was followed by another issue structured along the concept of *mushārakah mutanaqisah* by Sarawak Shell Bhd in 1991.[24] Buying out shares periodically has similarities with diminishing *mushārakah* due to its periodic share buy-back. This exit strategy is used as a benchmark for diminishing *mushārakah*, however there are difference between the two, especially when looking at the *Shari'ah* compliant issue. Figure 6.1 shows how diminishing *mushārakah* works in the venture capital scene.

The venture capital company goes into a partnership agreement with the investee company and the agreement will include the amount of shares that the investee may buy back from the venture capitalist in instalments. Using diminishing *mushārakah* as an exit strategy, the price per unit of the share cannot be fixed in the promise of the entrepreneur to purchase from the venture capital company, because whether the business is a success or not, the entrepreneur has to pay that amount. By right, the price is evaluated based on actual profit and on the invested company's value and performance. According to Mufti Taqi Usmani, if the price is fixed beforehand at the time of entering the *mushārakah*, it will practically mean that the client has ensured the principal invested by the financier with or without profit and this is prohibited in the case of *mushārakah*.[25]

According to Mufti Taqi Usmani, the financier can opt to price the share by agreeing to sell the units on the basis of valuation of the business at the time of purchase of each unit of the shares. If the value of the business has increased, the price will be higher and if it has decreased the price will be lower.[26] He also discusses the enforceability of the promise. He stated that there are a number of Muslim jurists who lecture that promises are enforceable, and that the court of law can compel the promisor to fulfil their promise, especially in the context of commercial activities. He also mentioned that some *Mālikī* and *Hanafī* jurists can be cited, in particular, who have declared that the promises can be enforced through courts of law in cases of need.

In terms of profitability, diminishing *mushārakah* appears to offer a moderate amount of profit, although the tiered diminishing *mushārakah* may be more profitable.[27] Diminishing *mushārakah* and share buyback are similar in the sense that shares are purchased by the entrepreneur. Given this similarity, some elements of the share buyback are used as a benchmark to analyse the applicability of diminishing *mushārakah* as an exit strategy. According to research in Malaysia, buying out shares can be applied in the venture capital based on these reasons:

- ability to obtain return target
- invested company has large amount of cash
- it can provide a win–win situation for the parties involved
- the objective and value extracted by the venture capitalist
- the financial instruments used, and
- the stage of the investment[28]

This shows that diminishing *mushārakah* can be applied as an exit strategy as long as the venture capital company can obtain the target return and, most importantly, the invested company has a large amount of cash. Invested companies would have more control of their business through purchasing their ownership from the venture capital companies.

Successful companies do not buy back their shares unless the invested company is not doing well, in which case they buy out their shares to add value to the company, although this may not necessarily increase the value significantly. However, payment based on payback of an equal amount and on a tiered basis can be an option for the diminishing *mushārakah* exit strategy. The tiered payments may increase the probability of the invested company and perhaps profitability for the venture capitalist.[29] In the case of the equal instalments this may not benefit the investors as it may limit their profitability and it is possible that the invested company may not be able to make payment at the beginning as it does not have a strong cash flow.[30]

It is only logical that venture capital companies will not let the entrepreneur exit at a price where they don't obtain higher return, especially when there is potential for higher value in the invested company in the long term. Furthermore, share buybacks may devalue the company due to higher flotation costs. However, if the entrepreneur is able to buy out at the highest market price, the venture capital company will accept the proposal. This shows the downside of diminishing *mushārakah*, whereby profit is limited. Although there are streams of payment during the first few years to the venture capital, it may not necessarily be as profitable an exit strategy for them as the sale from an IPO and trade sale can surpass the profitability of a diminishing *mushārakah*. However, this varies on a case-by-case basis and is dependent on the agreement between the venture capital company and the invested company.

On the contrary, the advantages of diminishing *mushārakah* and the buyback feature concentrate the equity in the hands of the entrepreneur. According to research by Cumming and Macintosh, buybacks are a partial exit, not a full exit.[31] The venture capitalist still holds some ownership of the invested company. This is not the case with the diminishing *mushārakah* where in the end the entrepreneur obtains full ownership of the company. For both diminishing *mushārakah* and buyback, equity is preferred as a medium of financing. For a buyback, the use of debt increases the agency cost of debt. In most cases it is high. This makes it difficult for further capital to be injected into the invested company. In the case of diminishing *mushārakah*, debt is not a *Shariʻah* permissible financial instrument as it bears interests. Information asymmetry is at the minimum for both methods because the buyer is the entrepreneur and information can be obtained easily by the entrepreneur and the investor. This helps to reduce valuation risk.[32]

In addition, debts may be used at the time when cash can't be raised by the entrepreneur for the buyback. Therefore, through diminishing *mushārakah*, it gives a venue for exiting via equity buyback without using debt and at the same time can create more value compared to a typical share buyback which appears as an inferior exit strategy compared to trade sales and IPO. Furthermore, the diminishing *mushārakah* can be an alternative for investments of moderate value class, which is far better than write-offs. To add the benefit of applying diminishing *mushārakah* as an exit strategy will be the transfer of control and ownership to the entrepreneur. This is stated in Black and Gilson's implicit contract theory, whereby IPOs and buybacks transfer control back to the entrepreneur, as the entrepreneur repurchases the venture capital interest.[33] This reduces information asymmetry and agency cost.

Diminishing *mushārakah* can be suitable for short-term investments as this reduces the risk for investors who have less of their capital tied up for a long period, and at the same time makes payments more affordable for the entrepreneur than having to make a lump sum payment on termination.[34] In addition, to exit through an IPO is costly and may not be worthwhile for a short-term investment. As for a trade sale, there is a risk that there may not be many potential buyers in the industry.

When it comes to applying diminishing *mushārakah* as an exit strategy, the financial instrument applied is in correlation with the exit strategy and the stage of the business, and ordinary shares are more appropriate in the later stage as compared to the early stage, which is highly risky. In the early stages, normally preference shares such as the convertible and the redeemable are used, as they provide the investors with a cushion for risk. The redeemable preference shares are appropriate to apply if the diminishing *mushārakah* is used as an exit strategy. Furthermore, through diminishing *mushārakah* it gives the entrepreneurs ownership of their company. This is stated in Cumming and Macintosh's study whereby buyback gives the firm's new owners both the incentive and the ability to monitor managers, because the new equity owners are the managers.[35]

Considering the investment stage, buying out shares as an exit strategy is more appropriate in the early stages due to the high level of risk at the start-up stage. Therefore diminishing *mushārakah* is more appropriately applied in the early stages and can be applied as an exit strategy. It is appropriate and viable for diminishing *mushārakah* to be applied as an exit mechanism for companies at the start-up stage because in the later stages invested companies have higher value and venture capital companies prefer to exit using other exit mechanisms that will provide them with a higher return. In the case of Malaysia, most of the investments are at the later stages, and therefore applying diminishing *mushārakah* is relatively viable for the early stage investments as an exit mechanism where risks are high.

Valuation and legal contracts are important when applying diminishing *mushārakah* as an exit strategy. A partnership is formed between the venture capital company and the investee company. Both will agree on the number of shares that the investee company will purchase. At this point the price per share cannot be fixed due to the uncertainty of the business being a success or not. Therefore, regardless of the business being successful or not, the investee company has to pay that amount. The price per share is evaluated based on company value and actual profit. This is based on the *mushārakah* principle which does not allow partners to prescribe to a fixed amount of profit at the beginning of the partnership.[36]

The study of diminishing *mushārakah* in the private equity and venture capital setting is still at its infancy. The potential of this profit–loss sharing instrument is yet to be explored and engineered to a degree of superior applicability in the finance industry as a whole, and not just in the area of Islamic banking and finance. The findings show that its applicability as an exit strategy has advantages for venture capital funding. Although it may not be a superior exit strategy compared to IPO and trade sale, it still has potential for lucrative returns for the investor and the entrepreneur, if the invested company has a solid amount of cash and is meeting target returns as negotiated between the venture capitalist and the invested company. Applying diminishing *mushārakah* also depends on the stage of investment, the financial instruments used and the valuation, legal contracts and procedures involved in making the deal.

It is recommended that diminishing *mushārakah* be applied as an exit mechanism for companies at the start-up stage because in the later stages invested companies have higher value and venture capital companies prefer to exit using other exit mechanisms that will provide them with higher return. Another recommendation for this study would be regarding establishing networks among angel investors. A group of investors or business angels who are experienced and have a lot of money will provide capital and knowledge in business to assist the entrepreneurs with their business management. With the diminishing *mushārakah* fund/exit strategy, a pool of angel investors can be established and it will be easier for the entrepreneurs to network with them. These angel investors can assist in establishing business at the seed and start-up stage. This study would build a platform for examining diminishing *mushārakah* as an exit strategy and financing tool in the private equity and venture capital industry in any country that has the infrastructure to use it. With the growth and expansion of the Islamic banking and finance industry, more financial instruments need to be explored and engineered.

6.4 Case studies

6.4.1 Asia: MESDAQ – providing the platform for Islamic venture capital growth

Investee companies in Malaysia can exit through MESDAQ which is responsible for improving the capital market in Malaysia. MESDAQ is focused specifically on growth and technology companies. MESDAQ is beneficial for

technology companies seeking investors. Through this listing the technology companies can have access to public
funds to assist in indigenous research development and to
develop Malaysia's science and technology industry.[37]

> According to the Malaysian Venture Capital Association and
> Private Equity Association (MVCA), about 30% of the com-
> panies listed on the MESDAQ Market last year were venture
> capital-backed. That says a lot because 2005 was a record year
> for MESDAQ IPOs (initial public offerings), with 46 new
> listings.[38]

Although this looks impressive there are many challenges
ahead in maintaining and improving IPO listing procedures.
Furthermore, it will be interesting to compare the growth
of investee companies funded by Islamic venture capital
with other venture capital-backed companies. In March
2008, the former Prime Minister of Malaysia, Dato' Seri
Abdullah bin Haji Ahmad Badawi, announced at the Invest
Malaysia 2008 Conference measures aimed at enhancing
the competitiveness and efficiency of the Malaysian equity
market.[39]

> The measures comprise, among others, the following: stream-
> lining of the current two boards on Bursa Malaysia Securities
> Berhad (Bursa Malaysia) to a new board by combining the
> Main Board and Second Board to form a unified board (UB)
> for more established corporations; expansion of the roles and
> objectives of the MESDAQ Market to facilitate growth corpo-
> rations to raise funds from the capital market (New MESDAQ);
> and adoption of a market-based regulatory approach for list-
> ing and fund-raising on the UB and New MESDAQ, prem-
> ised on adequacy of disclosures and corporate conduct of the
> corporations and promoters.[40]

This is an excellent move to spur growth within the venture capital and private equity industry whereby the market is expanded on a global scale. Following this,

> The SC [Securities Commission] intends to allow the listing of SPACs [special purpose acquisition companies] on Bursa Malaysia with a view to promoting private equity (PE) activities, spurring corporate transformation and encouraging mergers and acquisitions to enhance the depth, breadth and competitiveness of the Malaysian capital market.[41]

Although this sounds impressive there are many challenges ahead in maintaining and improving IPO listing procedures. Furthermore, it will be interesting to compare the growth of investee companies funded by Islamic venture capital with that of other venture capital-backed companies. This will also altogether benefit Islamic venture capital and *Shari'ah* compliant private equity.

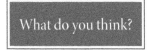

What do you think?

1. What are the major challenges that need to be addressed in developing the IPO market in Malaysia?
2. How would the New MESDAQ support local and foreign corporations in terms of fundraising? What are the opportunities?
3. Discuss the performance of other exit routes in Malaysia that can yield high return on investments.

6.4.2 *MENA: exit strategy challenges in the Middle East*

One of the challenges for developing Islamic private equity in the Middle East is the exit strategy. Applying the best exit strategy is vital to securing returns from the investment made. According to the article 'Opportunities in Islamic private equity', 'while US$6.5 billion has been invested by private equity firms since 1998, only 5% (US$0.3 billion) has been realized in exits.'[42] This is a big challenge for private equity companies in the Middle East and especially where Islamic private equity is concerned. Nevertheless, the IPO market in the GCC remains one of the most promising routes for private equity managers. According to the same article,

> Some notable exits include Injazat Technology Fund's sale of their investment in Atos Origin Middle East (AOME) through the sale of the company to HP, achieving a significant internal rate of return (IRR) of 75%. Also, Raya Holding, yielding a return of over 40 per cent for Injazat and was soon after listed on the Cairo Exchange. The most celebrated early exit for the industry was Abraaj Capital's sale of logistic company Aramex to Arab International Logistic for US$ 189 million in cash.[43]

Some of the constraints faced in establishing the MENA exit strategy include 'the scarcity of potential Islamic target portfolio companies and a lack of public market exit options, with most capital markets in Islamic banking centres seen as not being deep and liquid enough'.[44] Aside from developing the IPO market, there are other viable exit strategies such as trade sale, which can deliver high returns as well.

What do you think?

1. What are the major challenges that need to be addressed in developing the exit mechanism in the MENA region?

2. Is the IPO market the best exit strategy for investment funds established in the MENA region?
3. Discuss the performance of other exit routes in the MENA region.

6.4.3 *The United Kingdom and Europe: Islamic exit strategy*

The United Kingdom appears to be the leader in Europe in terms of innovation and market for Islamic banking and finance services. For example, Aston Martin and Amtech Power Software are two cases involving Islamic leveraged buyout. Furthermore, the United Kingdom's financial system and infrastructure is attractive for establishing Islamic banking and finance in Europe. To date the Islamic banking and finance industry in the UK provides products and services such as Islamic mortgages, Islamic asset management and Islamic private equity. There are several investment banks in the UK such as the European Islamic Investment bank and Gatehouse Bank who are active in innovating *Shari'ah* compliant instruments for Islamic exits and acquisition. From 'Sharia-compliant private equity: Old dog learns new tricks', examples of buyouts made in the UK include:

- July 2006: £15 million management buyout of UK-based computer software company, Amtech Power Software, thought to be the first Sharia-compliant management buyout in the UK.
- March 2007: £479 million buyout of Aston Martin by a group of Kuwaiti investors using Sharia-compliant murabaha (cost-plus financing) facility.
- May 2008: Management buyout of Downhole Products Limited, a Scottish manufacturer using a murabaha metals trading facility from Royal Bank of Scotland; a rare example of Sharia-compliant financing being provided directly

by a UK bank (offshore vehicles are usually used for tax and other commercial reasons).[45]

The buyout of Aston Martin used a *Shari'ah* compliant *murabaha*, however there are other modes of financing that can be used for this purpose, such as *ijara*, *mushārakah* and *mudharabah*. The UK has been quick to grasp the concept of *Shari'ah* law in the Islamic private equity sector, however tax legislation has to be altered to make Islamic banking and finance services attractive to investors.

What do you think?

1. What are the factors that make Islamic leveraged buyout in the United Kingdom successful?
2. Analyse the differences between leveraged buyout and Islamic leveraged buyout. Which one is more attractive to you as an investor?
3. What is the future market for Islamic leveraged buyout in the UK?
4. Discuss the future of Islamic leveraged buyout in the long run in terms of capital return.

6.4.4 *North America: Islamic private equity exit*

Guidance Financial Group, an international Islamic financial services company in the US, structured Asia's first Islamic buyout fund.[46] In September 2003, it announced the successful closing of Asia's first Islamic private equity fund and is also *Shari'ah* advisor to the fund.[47] Guidance Financial Group was the fund that was established in collaboration with Navis for the amount of US$86 million whereby it makes acquisitions of market-leading enterprises in well-established industries throughout Asia through management buyouts, management buy-ins, restructuring and recapitalisations.

What do you think?

1. What are the factors that make Islamic private equity in the United States successful?
2. Analyse the differences between management buyout and management buy-in. Which one is more attractive to you as an investor?
3. What is the future market for Islamic private equity in the United States?

Notes

1. *Participating Preferred Shares,* http://encyclopedia.thefreed-ictionary.com/Participating+Preferred+Shares (retrieved 10 November 2010).
2. Resolutions of the Securities Commission *Shari'ah* Advisory Council (Kuala Lumpur: Securities Commission, 2002), p. 71.
3. Companies Act 1965, Act 125, Section 4, Commissioner of Law Revision, Malaysia.
4. Resolutions of the Securities Commission *Shari'ah* Advisory Council, p. 72.
5. Ibid.
6. David Gladstone and Laura Gladstone, *Venture Capital Handbook: An Entrepreneur's Guide to Raising Venture Capital* (Englewood Cliffs: Prentice Hall, 2002), p. 17.
7. Rodney Wilson, 'Shariah compliant private equity finance', in Sohail Jaffer, *Islamic Wealth Management* (London: Euromoney Books, 2009), pp. 399–412.
8. Ibid. p. 408.

9. Chris Wright, 'The LBO hits Islamic finance – but how?', *Asiamoney*, March 2008.
10. Investopedia, 'IPO basics: what is an IPO?', http://www. investopedia.com/university/ipo/ipo.asp (retrieved 26 July 2010).
11. Bursa Malaysia Listing Requirements (n.d.), http://www. bursamalaysia.com/website/bm/regulation/rules/listing_ requirements/downloads/mesdaqmkt_listingreq2001.pdf (retrieved 16 April 2010).
12. Bursa Malaysia Listing Statistics (n.d.), http://www.bursa malaysia.com/website/bm/listed_companies/ipos/listing_ statistics.html (retrieved 16 April 2010).
13. *Management Buyout* (n.d.), http://www.valuebasedmanage ment.net/methods_management_buy-out.html (retrieved 26 July 2010).
14. Ibid.
15. Ibid.
16. Investopedia, 'Management buyout-MBO', http://www.inves topedia.com/terms/m/mbo.asp#axzz1x1DJCUko (retrieved 4 June 2012).
17. Investopedia, 'Management buy-in', http://www.investope dia.com/terms/m/mbi.asp (retrieved 4 June 2012).
18. The Free Dictionary, Management Buy-In, http://financial. dictionary.thefreedictionary.com/Management+Buy-In (retrieved 14 September 2010).
19. Investopedia, 'Mergers and acquisition', http://www.invest opedia.com/terms/m/mergersandacquisitions.asp#axzz 1x1DJCUko (retrieved 4 June 2012).
20. Rodney A. Wilson, 'The interface between Islamic and conventional banking', in Munawar Iqbal and David T. Llewellyn (eds), *Islamic Banking and Finance* (Cheltenham: Edward Elgar Publishing, 2002), p. 203.
21. Ibid. p. 204.
22. Abdul Rahim Abdul Rahman, 'Accounting regulatory issues

on investments in Islamic bonds', *International Journal of Islamic Financial Services*, 2002, vol. 4, no. 4, pp. 8–9.

23. Ibid. p. 8.

24. Nik Ramlah Mahmood, opening address to the Seminar on Islamic Private Debt Securities: Exploring New Opportunities in the Capital Market, 21 September 2001, http://www.sc.com. my/eng/html/resources/speech/sp_20010926.html (retrieved 24 September 2004).

25. Muhammad Taqi Usmani, *An Introduction to Islamic Finance* (Alphen aan den Rijn: Kluwer Law International, 2002), p. 92.

26. Ibid.

27. Wilson, 'Shariah compliant private equity finance', pp. 399–412.

28. Fara M. Ahmad Farid, *The Potential of Mushārakah as an Islamic Financial Structure for Venture Capital Funding in Malaysia*, Ph.D. thesis, Durham University, 2008.

29. Wilson, 'Shariah compliant private equity finance', pp. 399–412.

30 Ibid. p. 409.

31. Douglas J. Cumming and Jeffrey G. Macintosh, 'A cross country comparison of full and partial venture capital exits', Social Science Research Network Electronic Paper Collection, 2002, http://papers.ssrn.com/abstract=268557 (retrieved 3 May 2008).

32. Ibid. p. 13.

33. Bernard S. Black and Ronald J. Gilson, 'Venture capital and the structure of capital markets: banks versus stock markets', *Journal of Financial Economics*, 1998, vol. 47, pp. 243–77.

34. Wilson, 'Shariah compliant private equity finance', pp. 399–412.

35. Cumming and Macintosh, 'A cross country comparison'.

36. Usmani, *An Introduction to Islamic Finance*, p. 92.

37. Bursa Malaysia Listing Requirements (n.d.), http://www. bursamalaysia.com/website/bm/regulation/rules/listing_

requirements/downloads/mesdaqmkt_listingreq2001.pdf
(retrieved 16 April 2010).

38. Errol Oh, 'The Mesdaq VC factor', *The Star Online*, 30 September 2006, http://thestar.com.my/news/story.asp?file=/
2006/9/30/bizweek/15574760&sec=bizweek (retrieved 13 February 2010).

39. Securities Commission, Consultation Paper No. 1, 2009,
http://www.sc.com.my/clients/sccommy/Links/consultation
paper_20090206_web.pdf (retrieved 25 June 2010).

40. Ibid. p. 1.

41. Ibid. p. 2.

42. Rafi-uddin Shikoh, 'Opportunities in Islamic private equity',
http://dinarstandard.com/finance/opportunities-in-islamic-
private-equity (retrieved 21 February 2011).

43. Ibid.

44. Reuters, 'Fire sales, M&A to lift Islamic private equity', 1
September 2009, http://www.reuters.com/article/2009/09/01/
islamic-financial-privateequity-idUSKLR35728520090901
(retrieved 25 June 2010).

45. 'Sharia-compliant private equity: old dog learns new tricks',
24 June 2008, http://finance.practicallaw.com/0-382-2651
(retrieved 9 June 2010).

46. Salahuddin Ahmed, *Islamic Banking and Insurance: A Global
Overview* (Kuala Lumpur: AS Noordeen, 2006), pp. 384–5.

47. Ibid. p. 385.

CHAPTER 7

TRUST, MONITORING METHODS AND DUE DILIGENCE

Defining trust in the context of Islamic venture capital and *Shari'ah* compliant private equity is to look at how trust can be nurtured and established between investors and entrepreneurs. It is hard to define 'trust' as it depends on what the investors are interested in with the investment deal. Aside from establishing trust, due diligence is part of the venture capital process whereby 'due diligence simply means that the investor must conduct background checks on the management team, complete an industry study, and verify the representations in [a] business proposal'.[1] Monitoring is also an important process in the venture capital cycle and helps managers to assist the entrepreneur in business decisions and company performance. All of the above are vital elements when it comes to developing the Islamic venture capital and *Shari'ah* compliant private equity industry.

7.1 Definitions of trust

'Trustworthiness' is looked for in an entrepreneur as well as skills to realise the business plan. A high level of trust between the venture capital and private equity companies and the entrepreneur may reduce the risk of moral hazard. This increases confidence in the relationship between both parties. Confidence can be achieved through trust-building mechanisms and an excellent level of control between the entrepreneur and the venture capitalist.[2] Trust can be in many forms, for example in the entrepreneurs' management skills, in the personality of the entrepreneur, transparency and corporate governance. Trust is hard to measure; however it is important in a *Shari'ah* compliant private equity and Islamic venture company in overcoming moral hazard and information asymmetry issues.

In my survey and research, the 'personality' category relates to characteristics as listed below to signify that the investees are trustworthy. For example:

- trustworthy
- fair
- sincere
- honest
- of high integrity
- straightforward
- dedicated[3]

These characteristics are also some of those listed by the venture capitalist before choosing an investment.[4] Trust is also defined as good corporate governance:

- transparency
- protecting shareholders' interest
- good reputation
- mutually agreed rights and responsibilities for all parties to establish a partnership that practises integrity and transparency

The example gives an idea of the kind of character that defines trust in a more narrow perspective. The focus is also on the agreement in this case and must be understood by the parties involved in terms of their rights and responsibilities. Every single detail of the transaction is documented. Therefore, trust needs to be enforced and empowered and this leads to methods of strengthening trust. To strengthen trust, the venture capital company focuses on transparency, a good relationship with the entrepreneur, cooperation, interaction and mutual understanding. There is a need to have an agreement to strengthen trust and enhance transparency in the operations and communication between the entrepreneur and the venture capital company.

Having a good relationship between the entrepreneur and the venture capitalist strengthens trust. In relation to strengthening trust, cooperation and interaction will add value not only to the investment but also to the relationship between the venture capitalist and the entrepreneur, as mentioned above. Value adding can strengthen trust as it shows that both parties are willing to cooperate and this is in line with the spirit of *mushārakah* (the basis for *Shari'ah* compliant private equity and Islamic venture capital) whereby it is based on the concept of *tawa'un* (cooperation). Conflicts of interest should be managed properly and the problems encountered discussed.

In terms of mutual understanding, to strengthen trust, the entrepreneur and the venture capital company need to establish an understanding that success is shared and thus this refers to the profit- and loss-sharing features in a partnership from an Islamic point of view. This mutual understanding shows that both have responsibility towards each other.

Trust is an important element in the partnership contract that is established in Islamic venture capital and *Shari'ah* compliant private equity. Furthermore, this is vital in the due diligence process where the venture capital company assesses the level of trustworthiness and personality of the potential entrepreneur. A high level of trustworthiness between the venture capitalist and the entrepreneur may reduce the risk of moral hazard and adverse selection.

7.2 Monitoring investments and due diligence

7.2.1 *Monitoring* Shari'ah *compliant private equity and venture capital funds*

In the case of a *Shari'ah* compliant private equity fund and Islamic venture capital, monitoring methods have to ensure that the businesses are operating according to *Shari'ah* guidelines and are based on the ISO standards (Islamic) when producing or manufacturing *halal* products. In the case of a *Shari'ah* compliant private equity and Islamic venture capital fund, it must be monitored to make sure that the invested companies follow the *Shari'ah* guidelines in terms of accounting reports based on AAOIFI standards.

In this case, the personnel in the company and the venture capital companies cannot depend on *Shari'ah* advisors only to advise them: the personnel themselves must be well versed in the *Shari'ah* guidelines and the *muamalat* principles that persist in transactions that emerge in an Islamic financial institution, which are the responsibility of the *Shari'ah* scholars in the *Shari'ah* Advisory Council in the Securities Commission Malaysia.

Malaysia's Islamic Banking Act 1983 provides for the licensing and regulation of Islamic banking businesses. The Act includes provisions on the financial requirements and duties of an Islamic bank, the ownership, control and management of Islamic banks, restrictions on their business, powers of supervision and control over Islamic banks, and other general provisions such as penalties.[5] There is also an ordinant under Malaysian Civil Law addressing legal cases that involve Islamic financial institutions.

7.2.2 Monitoring methods

The process of monitoring investments and the invested company is carried out to ensure that the business runs efficiently and also to ensure the efficiency of the risk management process in *Shari'ah* compliant private equity and Islamic venture capital companies. Monitoring is carried out to anticipate and avoid problems in a timely manner.[6] Based on my survey and research, examples of monitoring methods include:

- board representation
- meetings
- site visits
- working committees
- appointing a senior officer for the annual general meeting and general meeting
- financial and business progress reporting (monthly accounts and yearly audited accounts)
- regular research into the industry and the company to examine progress[7]

Venture capital companies are more active as compared to banks when it comes to monitoring a business. This adds value to the management and the investment team for the investee companies.

7.2.3 Due diligence process

Most ventures are new and the entrepreneurs may lack experience. Therefore a complicated, proper evaluation is neither possible nor desirable. The venture capitalist therefore relies on a subjective evaluation. The venture capitalist evaluates the quality of the entrepreneur before appraising the characteristics of the product, market or technology. Therefore, before making a commitment some due diligence process has to be completed. This is the third stage in the venture capital process.

The venture capitalist is reviewing the entrepreneur, their company and the industry in a thorough study. The venture capitalist is looking for potential in the entrepreneur, management team, product and the industry, not forgetting the potential of the company to make money. In this due diligence process, the venture capitalist visits a company to see how the business is doing; this is for existing businesses and not start-ups. Other than this, individual or the entrepreneur's track records such as credit checks are investigated to ensure that he comes from a good business background. After thorough investigation and evaluation, the venture capitalist closes the deal with legal documents.

After closing the deal, the final stage of the venture capital process is on working together with the venture capital companies and this is similar to a business partner, whereby all major policy decisions should be discussed with them. It is also at this stage that trust is built and harnessed. The venture capital companies have the knowledge and experience and can guide the entrepreneur, although the entrepreneur is responsible for the day-to-day operations. At this stage the venture capital company requires monthly reports from the entrepreneur so as to monitor his progress. It is also important that the entrepreneur holds board meetings with the venture capitalist to keep them updated with the business's progress. Sometimes a venture capitalist appoints a member into the company's board of directors to monitor the business.

In this matter both the entrepreneur and the venture

capital company have their own appointed lawyer to close the deal. These legal documents cover what is expected from the entrepreneur and the responsibilities of the venture capital company and describe the sale of stock and the price being paid. The legal documents show that every aspect of the investment is covered, ensuring a long-lasting relationship.

Notes

1. David Gladstone and Laura Gladstone, *Venture Capital Handbook: An Entrepreneur's Guide to Raising Venture Capital* (Englewood Cliffs: Prentice Hall, 2002), p. 356.

2. D. A. Shepherd and A. L. Zacharakis, 'The venture capitalist–entrepreneur relationship: control, trust and confidence in co-operative behaviour', *An International Journal of Entrepreneurial Finance*, 2001, vol. 3, no. 2, pp. 129–49.

3. Fara M. Ahmad Farid, *The Potential of Mushārakah as an Islamic Financial Structure for Venture Capital Funding in Malaysia*, Ph.D. thesis, Durham University, 2008.

4. Ibid. p. 260.

5. Lawyerment.com.my, 'Your guide to Malaysian legal information: Financial law – Banking Law: Islamic Banking Act 1983' (n.d.), http://www.lawyerment.com.my/financial/banking.shtml (retrieved 17 October 2005).

6. W. A. Sahlman, 'The structure and governance of venture capital organisations', *Journal of Financial Economics*, vol. 27, 1990, pp. 473–521.

7. Farid, *The Potential of Mushārakah.*

GLOSSARY

bai al-arbun   down payment on a sales contract. The full price of the goods purchased is not fully paid and the buyer has not taken possession of the goods. If the buyer does not purchase the goods, the down payment will be forfeited

bai al-inah   refers to the selling of an asset by the bank to the customer through deferred payments. At a later date, the bank will repurchase the asset

bai al-istisna   contract for manufacturing (or construction) whereby the manufacturer (seller) agrees to provide the buyer with goods identified by description after they have been manufactured (or constructed) in conformity with that description within a pre-determined timeframe and price

bai al-salam   contract whereby payment is done in advance and the goods delivered later. According to *Shari'ah* law, the goods have to be in existence while transactions take place. However, in the case of the *salam* financing there are some exceptions

diminishing musharakah   'equity sharing' Islamic financing technique used for financing projects. It uses different types of profit and loss sharing partnerships. Shares are purchased periodically

177

	from the financier until the borrower fully owns the asset
fiqh	Islamic jurisprudence
gharar	risk, uncertainty and hazard
ghubn	price deception. This can give the option to the seller to cancel the contract if they discover that the price is higher than the market price
hadith	record of the sayings, deeds or tacit approvals of Prophet Muhammad (pbuh)
halal	permitted by Islam
Hanafi	one of the four schools of thought in Islam
Hanbali	one of the four schools of thought in Islam
haram	prohibited by Islam
hawalah	contract consisting of transfer of debt from one party to another. This transfer is via an intermediary
ijarah	medium-term mode of financing which involves purchasing and subsequently transferring the right of use of the equipment and machinery to the beneficiary for a specific period of time
ijarah wa iqtina	leasing type of financing mode with the option to purchase the asset by the lessee at the end of the leasing period
istisna	contract whereby both parties agree in manufacturing goods and commodities. The payment is made in advance and the goods and commodities delivered at a future date. Payments can be made in instalments as agreed by the parties involved
'iwad	equivalent counter value in exchange

juala (commission)	contract to assign a task to another party who agrees to carry out the task agreed with a commission or a fee
Mālikī	one of the four schools of thought in Islam
muamalat	sub-division of *Shari'ah*, meaning interactions and transactions
mudhārabah	mode of business where two or more persons participate: one (or some) with capital and the other (or others) with labour and enterprise. The financier shares the profit with the entrepreneur according to mutually agreed terms. In the case of loss, it is borne by the financier alone
murabaha	a sale contract whereby an Islamic financial institution sells a good to a client who makes deferred payments including a profit markup. The Islamic financial institution may have already acquired the good, or may acquire the good from the supplier on behalf of the client once the contract is signed
mushārakah	mode of business in which more than one person joins with capital and labour on the basis of profit and loss sharing, the profit rate being agreed by the partners
rahn	to pledge a property that has value as a security for debt. The creditor will recover the debt from the property in case the debtor cannot pay back in time
riba	pre-determined increase on the amount of loan which increases over time. It is equivalent to interest
riba al-buyu'i	*riba* that occurs on the exchange of goods and involves payments

riba al-fadhli	selling of *ribawi* items whereby excess is taken in exchange of specific homogeneous items through hand-to-hand purchase
riba al-nasi'ah	selling of different *ribawi* items on deferred terms. When the goods arrive and the seller cannot pay for them, the tenure is added together with the addition in payment
riba al-qardhi	contract on debt or loan for a specified tenure and additional payment on the debt or loan
riba al-yad	selling or exchange of different *ribawi* items in cash where either one of the goods is delivered later
ribawi	relating to *riba*
salam	sale where the seller undertakes to supply some specific goods to the buyer at a future date in exchange for an agreed price fully paid at spot
Shāfi'ī	one of the four schools of thought in Islam
Shari'ah	Islamic law from the Al-Quran and also from the examples and lifestyle of Prophet Muhammad (pbuh), the *sunnah*
shirkah al-amlak	partnership in property
shirkah al-inan	two or more people pool their capital, work together and share the profits
shirkah al-mufawadah	partners combine in every type of *shirkah*, namely *al-inan*, *al-wujuh* and *al-abdan*
shirkah al-'uqud	partnership in contracts (plural *shirkah-ul-'aqd*)
shirkah al-wujuh	partnership in credit: one or more of the partners procures goods on credit, sells them and shares/distributes the profit

shirkah-ul-'aqd	partnership in business affected by mutual contract
shirkah ul-milk	joint ownership between two or more partners in a particular property
shirkat-ul-a'mal	partners jointly undertake to render some services for their customers and the fee charged is distributed among the partners on an agreed ratio. Also called *shirkat-ut-taqabbul, shitkat-us-sana'i'* or *shirkat-ul-abdan.*
shirkat-ul-amwal	partners invest some capital into a commercial enterprise
shirkat-ul-wujooh	in this type of *shirkah* the partners have no investment. They purchase the commodities at a deferred price and sell them on the spot. The profit earned is distributed between them at an agreed ratio.
sukuk	asset-backed bond designed or structured in accordance with *Shari'ah* that may be traded in the market
sunnah	the normative behaviour of Prophet Muhammad (pbuh) as evidenced by his utterances and his tacit approvals
takaful	Islamic insurance based on a pooling system to aid and to guarantee each other from damages and losses
taqwa	piety; an essential trait of the character of a Muslim, it encompasses a number of values such as honesty, thankfulness to God, remembering God, justice, benevolence and spending in the way of God
urf	referring to the custom, or 'knowledge', of a given society, leading to change in the *fiqh*

wadiah	customers deposit money in the bank and the bank is totally responsible and liable for its safekeeping. It is safekeeping with guarantee. Commonly used in Islamic banks in Malaysia
wakalah	contract of agency whereby one is appointed to carry out a certain task by the contractor (banks). For example, mutual funds and brokerage services who are the agent (*wakil*) for the Islamic banks
wakil	agent (to act on behalf)
zakat	amount payable by a Muslim on their net wealth as a part of their religious obligation, mainly for the benefit of the poor and the needy. Levied at the rate of 2.5 per cent on all financial assets and stock-in-trade of business; at 10 per cent on agricultural produce of rain-irrigated cultivation; and at 5 per cent on the produce of artificially irrigated cultivation. Payable at different rates on livestock reared for sale. The exemption limits are quite low, so it has a very wide coverage.

INDEX